KU-283-962

A CREATIVE STEP-BY-STEP GUIDE TO

HEATHERS AND
CONIFERS

A CREATIVE STEP-BY-STEP GUIDE TO

HEATHERS AND
CONIFERS

Author
Sue Phillips

Photographer
Neil Sutherland

AURA BOOKS

CLB 4665
This edition published in 1997 by Aura Books
© 1996 CLB International, Godalming, Surrey
Printed and bound in Singapore
All rights reserved
ISBN 0-94779-321-6

Credits

Edited, designed and typeset by Ideas into Print
Photographs: Neil Sutherland
Production Director: Gerald Hughes
Production: Ruth Arthur, Sally Connolly, Neil Randles,
Paul Randles, Karen Staff

THE AUTHOR

Sue Phillips began gardening at the age of four, encouraged
by her grandfather, and had her first greenhouse at eleven,
where she grew a collection of cacti and propagated all
sorts of plants. After leaving school, she worked for a year
on a general nursery before studying horticulture at
Hadlow College of Agriculture & Horticulture, Kent for
three years. For the next five years, she was co-owner and
manager of a nursery in Cambridgeshire, before joining a
leading garden products company as Gardens Adviser. This
involved answering gardening queries, handling
complaints, writing articles and press releases, speaking at
gardening events and broadcasting for local radio. In 1984,
she turned freelance and since then she has contributed
regularly to various gardening and general interest
magazines and has appeared often on radio and TV. She is
the author of several published books. She lives in a very
windy village on the south coast of England near
Chichester and has a very intensively cultivated cottage
garden on solid clay, plus a vegetable garden next door,
which she looks after with help from her husband and
hindrance from a Persian cat.

THE PHOTOGRAPHER

Neil Sutherland has more than 25 years experience in a
wide range of photographic fields, including still-life,
portraiture, reportage, natural history, cookery, landscape
and travel. His work has been published in countless books
and magazines throughout the world.

Half-title page: Chamaecyparis lawsoniana ‘Minima Aurea’.
Title page: Creating a miniature garden with compact
conifers and rock plants in a sink.
Copyright page: Erica carnea ‘Springwood Pink’ and a
prostrate juniper glistening with frost.

CONTENTS

CLASSIC PLANTS FOR MODERN GARDENS

The first conifers were primitive plants that inhabited the earth about 150 million years ago, long before conventional flowering plants evolved, with their brightly colored petals needing insects to pollinate them. (Conifers do indeed produce flowers, but they are normally inconspicuous, being pollinated by the wind). Conifers grow all over the world's surface apart from the hottest regions; you will not find them in rain forest and desert areas. There are species adapted to hot dry climates, and others to extremely cold climates; a few are specially adapted to survive in waterlogged soil. But most, in the wild, make big trees.

The majority of the dwarf conifers we grow in gardens arose as a result of spontaneous mutations that appeared in the branches of big trees as clusters of compact, stunted shoots known as 'witches brooms'. By propagating from these, often grafting them onto suitable rootstocks, a huge range of garden worthy conifers have been generated. Today there are more than ever, with new cultivars appearing in nurseries and garden centers continuously. Since conifers often grow wild with heather, and the two enjoy similar conditions in gardens, it became the fashion some years ago to associate the two together to create easy-care, all-year-round gardens. Fashions in gardening come and go, but now conifers and heathers are in great demand for containers, patios, and low-maintenance beds all over the world.

Left: *Mature heather and conifers beds on a grand scale.*   **Above:** *Heather colors range from white to purple.*

Planting a conifer

Once well-established, conifers are generally trouble-free and easy to look after, but it is worth taking trouble over their planting and initial care. Newly planted conifers often fail simply because the soil around them dries out too much or the foliage is desiccated by harsh drying winds. Both conditions can cause the foliage to turn brown; at best, young plants will be left with spoiled foliage that may never be replaced with fresh green growth, and at worst they die. The secret of successful conifer planting is to prepare the soil very well first. It should be moisture-retentive, but not waterlogged. Early fall and late spring are the best time to plant conifers, along with other evergreens, but plants grown in pots can be planted out during the rest of the year, too, as long as the soil is in reasonable condition and neither too hot and dry nor too cold and wet. Although conifers are often recommended for growing as windbreaks, they must become well established before being subjected to drying winds, so it is good practice to surround them with a temporary windbreak. Feeding is not the main priority after planting; once plants have made it through the first winter, sprinkle a light dose of general-purpose feed or a special formulation for conifers around the plant and water it in well.

2 Remove the conifer from its pot and lower it into the hole. There is no need to ease out the roots unless the plant is severely potbound. Check that the plant is upright and that its best side, if any, faces front.

Before planting a conifer, make sure that the hole is free of weeds, roots and debris. Time spent on preparation ensures that conifers get off to a good start.

1 Fork well-rotted organic matter, such as garden compost or manure, into the soil over the entire bed. Dig a hole that is slightly bigger than the rootball of the plant.

3 Fill in round the roots with the surrounding improved topsoil, taking care not to put the plant in too deep. The top of the rootball should be barely covered by soil.

4 If the rootball is bone dry, stand the whole plant in a bucket of water for an hour or until the bubbles stop rising, before planting. After planting, water in very thoroughly.

5 Apply a deep mulch of bark chippings or similar material to retain moisture in the soil. If allowed to dry out, newly planted conifers turn brown and are unlikely to recover.

6 As an added precaution - vital in exposed areas - surround newly planted conifers with a windbreak to protect them from strong winds, which can kill them.

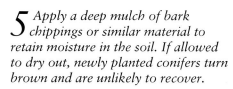

7 Conifers planted in the fall are most at risk, since the weather is windiest then. The windbreak must be securely fixed, but need only be left in place for the first winter.

The windbreak can be made of perforated plastic sheet, as here, or hessian, interwoven fabric or sheep hurdles.

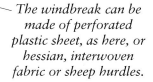

Above: *A mixed border of conifers and heathers give year-round interest with some seasonal changes. Varying shapes, sizes and colors contribute to a pleasing, easy-care landscape.*

Routine cultivation

Providing you have bought healthy plants, improved the soil with organic matter and/or grit as necessary before planting, and protected the plants from wind and drying out immediately afterwards, conifers and heathers virtually look after themselves. Routine cultivation is limited to normal garden care, such as weeding, watering in dry spells and occasional feeding. Hand weeding is preferable to hoeing, since heathers and many conifers - dwarf types in particular - have shallow roots that are easily damaged. Regular weeding is particularly important, as conifers and heathers need plenty of direct sun and a smothering blanket of weeds soon cuts out the light, causing stems and branches to die back. Keeping weeds down also cuts down competition for water during dry spells, which again is important to stop conifer and heather foliage from turning brown.

   To help retain moisture, it is a good idea to clear weeds from conifer and heather beds in spring, when the soil is naturally moist, and mulch with 1-2in(2.5-5cm) of well-rotted organic matter, such as garden compost. This also helps to smother out germinating weed seedlings. For best results, apply a mulch after sprinkling on a spring feed of general fertilizer; this way, the moisture present in the soil will be sufficient to dissolve solid fertilizers, making them available to the plants. (In summer or when soil is dry, liquid or soluble fertilizers are better; these are also the feeds to use for conifers and heathers in containers.) Choose a formulation containing plenty of trace elements or apply a liquid seaweed feed to promote good color development in conifer and heather foliage - especially the red- and gold-leaved kinds.

   As a general rule, conifers do not need pruning. Clip hedges and topiary specimens tightly once or twice a year. Check specimen plants periodically - especially prostrate kinds, which occasionally produce strong upright shoots. To keep the plant tidy, remove wayward or out-of-place shoots whenever you see them.

1 Choose a healthy plant with no brown foliage. Whether the plant is to go into a container or out into the garden, check a few basic points first when you get it home.

2 Moss or liverwort growing on the potting mixture around the plant can be a sign that the plant has been in the same pot for some time and may be running short of feed.

Soaking the rootball

1 If plants are bone dry, the pot probably feels unusually light. Soak the rootball before planting, or it will not grow away well.

2 Leave the plant in its pot and submerge the entire rootball in a bucket of water. Wait till the bubbles stop and allow to drain.

3 Scrape moss or liverwort away carefully using an old fork; remove any weeds at the same time. If the soil surface seems very compressed, loosen it slightly with the prongs of the fork.

Soluble feed for acid-loving plants. Dissolve the crystals in water and use regularly during the growing season.

Granular sequestered iron supplies iron in a fast-acting, easily assimilated form. Ericaceous plants need iron, which is chemically locked up by any lime in the soil. If lime is present, plant leaves turn yellow due to iron deficiency.

Feeding ericaceous plants

Different kinds of feed are available for ericaceous plants. Use soluble crystals to feed plants and to help acidify the soil. Use solid ericaceous fertilizer to improve the soil before planting or around established plants. Sequestered iron is a 'tonic' for ericaceous plants. There is also a liquid version that needs diluting before use; this is best for pots.

Solid ericaceous fertilizer. Scatter it on the soil and water in well. Use each year in spring and to improve soil before planting.

1 After spring weeding, sprinkle fertilizer on moist soil around individual plants, or thinly between plants in an ericaceous bed.

4 Loosen any dense-packed roots out from the mass, but without breaking or skinning them. The bottom of the rootball will be loosest.

5 Finally, tease a few of the biggest roots out slightly from the rootball before planting; this allows roots to start growing outwards into the soil.

2 Gently work the fertilizer into the top 1-2in(2.5-5cm) of soil with a small hand cultivator. Avoid going too deep or you may damage the shallow roots of heathers and other ericaceous plants.

3 Finish off with a mulch 1-2in (2.5-5cm) deep over all the exposed soil. Bark or wood chippings, or cocoa shell (as used here) look best in heather and conifer beds.

1 *After digging, fertilizing and raking the bed level, spread a layer of moss peat or other organic matter over it to improve the soil. This helps it to hold both water and air, thus aiding root development.*

2 *Fork the peat into the top of the soil. As conifers and heathers are relatively shallow rooted, improving the surface helps to retain moisture around the roots and 'backs up' the effect of mulching later.*

3 *After deciding the positions of the plants - perhaps standing them, still in their pots, on the bed - begin planting. Start with the biggest or most important plants. Knock them out of their pots, taking care not to break up the rootballs.*

Making a conifer and heather bed

Heathers and conifers naturally associate well together and need the same conditions - sun, neutral or acid soil that neither dries out nor becomes waterlogged, and an open site with plenty of fresh air. Both can be grown in traditional beds and borders, but one of the newer ways to plant them is in island beds - informal shapes such as 'teardrops' cut out of the lawn. Being open on all sides, such beds are very easy to weed, and much more light and air can reach the plants, which tend to be healthier and rarely bothered by pests. The secret of an attractive heather and conifer bed lies in teaming plants with highly contrasting shapes, colors and textures. Upright, flame- and dome-shaped conifers contrast with open branching or bushy shapes, and all are set off well by a continuous carpet of heather underneath. Choose heathers from all the main groups, so that you can have something in flower virtually the whole year round and use a few conifers with colored foliage, with colored tips to young foliage in spring, or that take on bronzey hues in winter for seasonal variation. Improving the soil before planting such a long-term bed is well worthwhile; use plenty of organic matter, and if the soil is not naturally acid use an acidic soil improver such as sphagnum moss peat, though this is not enough to turn chalky soil into one suitable for most heathers.

Calluna vulgaris
'Silver Knight'

Juniperus communis
'Compressa'

Erica cinerea
'Sherry'

Calluna vulgaris
'Tib'

4 Space the conifers, allowing for the size they will reach in ten years; see the plant label. Surround them with heathers spaced about 12-18in(30-45cm) apart; these should make a complete carpet within two years.

5 Water all the plants very thoroughly. If the pots are dry when you buy them, soak the roots for a few hours before planting so that the rootball gets wet right through.

6 Finish with a decorative mulch to help retain moisture. This cocoa shell looks very good with this type of planting. Cocoa shell is slightly acidic, and the chocolate smell deters cats.

7 The finished bed requires very little maintenance. Top up the mulch each spring and feed the plants at the same time. Water new plants during dry spells for the first summer.

17

Plants to grow with heathers and conifers

Below: *Plants with tall or spiky shapes or large rounded leaves make good contrasts with both heathers and conifers, and look good grown together in groups among them. It does not take many such groups to soften the effect and to add touches of seasonal variation.*

A heather bed, even one augmented with conifers, evergreens and birches, looks more interesting with areas of contrasting small plants to ring the changes. Clearly the plants you choose must enjoy heather bed conditions - sunny, well-drained and lime-free - but they should also contribute a range of shapes, colors and textures that will contrast well with heathers. Grasses, distinctively shaped herbaceous plants and miniature shrubs are good choices. The grasses can range from 10ft(3m)- tall *Miscanthus*, through medium-sized *Helictotrichon* to dwarf rockery types such as *Festuca*, not forgetting the ornamental sedges, such as *Carex morrowii* 'Evergold', that like well-drained conditions. Evergreen grasses are most effective for long-term display, but it is worth including some that die down in winter, such as Bowle's golden sedge *(Carex elata* 'Aurea'), for their bright colors. Choose tall waving grasses, such as *Stipa gigantea,* which looks like giant oats, and *Miscanthus* 'Silver Feather', with its pampaslike plumes, to add movement to an otherwise still scene. For herbaceous plants, choose those with striking shapes and colors; drifts of *Bergenia, Ophiopogon* and *Liriope muscari* or clumps of *Liatris, Galtonia* and *Asphodelus*. If you feel experimental, consider unusual associations, such as heathers with red hot pokers or the giant artichoke *Cynara scolymus, Nandina domestica* 'Firepower' (heavenly bamboo), yucca and cordyline palms, or the huge crinkly leaved *Crambe cordifolia,* which has masses of gypsophila-like flower in summer. On rockeries or in raised beds, compact heather cultivars and dwarf conifers associate well with many kinds of alpines, but avoid adding heathers to a conventional flower garden, as the two don't 'go'.

Liatris spicata

Yucca filamentosa 'Bright Edge'

Bergenia cordifolia

Below: Linear shapes associate particularly well with heathers and conifers; choose plants with strong colors and robust stems to create a bold effect. Mix evergreens with plants such as Molinia, *which bring in seasonal highlights to make the most of a display.*

Miscanthus sinensis 'Zebrinus' (tiger grass)

Molinia caerulea 'Variegata'

Phormium tenax 'Rainbow Maiden'

Pieris 'Forest Flame'

Vaccinium vitis-idaea 'Koralle'

Azalea 'Salmon's Leap'

Shrubs for acid soil

Acid-loving plants team particularly well with heathers and conifers growing on acid or lime-free soil. Variegated plants, such as Azalea 'Salmon's Leap' and plants that flower and fruit such as Vaccinium vitis-idaea 'Koralle', with white flowers in spring and large deep red berries in late summer, are particularly valuable. Pieris 'Forest Flame' has spring flowers and bright red new growth.

Suitable companions

Plants with fruit or berries plus evergreen leaves: Arbutus unedo, Gaultheria *and* Skimmia.
Flowers: Crinodendron hookerianum, Desfontainia spinosa, Embothrium, Enkianthus, Fabiana, Hamamelis, Kalmia,
Autumn foliage: Blueberry, Fothergilla,
Spring bracts: Cornus canadensis, C. florida, and C. kousa. Pieris.
Dwarf deciduous shrubs: Betula nana *(birch),* Salix boydii *and* S. lanata *(willows).*

Problem solving

Compared to many garden plants, conifers are fairly trouble-free. The biggest single cause of problems is drying out, which can happen at almost any stage, although young plants are most at risk. Newly planted conifers that turn completely brown within a few weeks or months of planting have usually died from wind 'scorching' the foliage. (High wind speeds cause the plant to lose water through its leaves faster than it can take it in through the roots.) Another frequent cause of early loss is drying out at the roots, usually caused if plants are dry when first planted. In this case, the ball of roots is bone dry inside and even watering after planting is not enough to rewet the compressed ball of roots and peat. To avoid these problems, soak dry plants and tease open a potbound rootball slightly, plant into well improved soil and shelter new plants with a windbreak for the first winter. Older plants can also be affected by browning. Dry soil is the usual cause; in this case, only the lower parts of the plant are usually affected and, though disfigured, it does not die. Watering and improving the soil by mulching each spring with organic matter or bark chippings would prevent the problem, but once it has occurred, the brown foliage will never revert to green. The best solution is disguise. Either plant climbing ivies or euonymus over the brown foliage or plant evergreen shrubs in front of the affected plant. Bear in mind that some conifers are less tolerant of exposure than others, so make sure that any susceptible plants are given a sheltered site, otherwise this, too, can be a cause of browning in future.

Above: Rhizoctonia root rot is occasionally a problem with heathers, causing affected plants to turn brown as if dry, and die off, often a few stems at a time. It is most common where soils lie wet in winter.

Dog damage

1 Dogs repeatedly lifting their legs over a conifer can cause it to turn brown towards the base on one side. Wash down the plant with plain water immediately.

2 Use an animal repellent in the form of granules, gels, powders, such as cat pepper, and tie-on capsules. Renew them frequently, especially after rain, for best effect.

1 *Dry soil is the commonest cause of basal browning in conifers. In the case of aging horizontal junipers, as shown here, entire branches sometimes die off, leaving the remaining plant looking normal.*

Most of this healthy green branch can be retained.

2 *You can improve the plant by removing entire brown branches - cut back to a junction with a healthy green stem. Replacing the plant is probably the best long-term solution.*

3 *The exposed soil will be full of old needles and rather impoverished; clear the debris, fork in plenty of well-rotted organic matter and a dressing of fertilizer. Replant with conifers or shrubs.*

Right: *When odd branches die back producing a cinnamon color, it is often a sign of a plant disease called phytophthora. The damage spreads slowly to other branches until the whole plant is killed - removing affected branches rarely prevents the spread of the disease and there is no cure. The best remedy is to dig out and destroy affected plants. Plants growing on waterlogged soils are most often affected.*

Pest problems

Conifers are fairly pest-free, but watch for two particular problems. Spider mites are very tiny insects that mainly affect dwarf conifers with dense leaves. They cause the foliage to go yellow or bronze towards the shoot tips; in severe cases, minute webs can be seen and needles drop. Spruce aphids are long lean 'greenfly' tucked in among the needles, especially of blue spruces. Check plants regularly for both problems in spring and summer; spray with a systemic garden pesticide (shown below) to eradicate them.

Winter-flowering heathers

Winter-flowering heathers are valuable and versatile garden 'finds'. They provide a carpet of evergreen, naturally compact, trouble-free ground cover that is full of flower throughout the winter. Unlike other heathers, they do not even need acid soil. Any reasonably well-drained garden soil in an open situation and full sun suits them; the soil may be acid, neutral or slightly alkaline, but add plenty of well-rotted organic matter before planting. The best-known winter heather is *Erica carnea*, which has a large range of readily available cultivars. Some have colored foliage, but other members of the heather family are better in this respect. Also available, but with a far smaller choice of cultivars, are *Erica mediterranea* and *E.* x *darleyensis*. Winter-flowering heathers associate superbly with conifers and the winter stems of birches, dogwoods, pollarded willows and *Rubus cockburnianus*. Evergreen shrubs team well with heathers, too; go for the more architectural kinds, such as *Viburnum rhytidophyllum* and *V. davidii*, those with berries or fruit, such as *Skimmia reevesiana* and *Arbutus unedo*, or ones with colored foliage, such as *Choisya ternata* 'Sundance'. Since the height of their display season occurs between late fall and early spring, a bed of winter-flowering heathers will also benefit from other seasonal interest. Go for plants with strong complementary shapes, such as brooms, and herbaceous plants with distinctive forms, such as bergenia and grasses. The result will be a highly attractive, yet low-maintenance, all-year-round garden.

Pruning winter heathers

As soon as the flowers start to turn brown at the end of the flowering season, around mid-spring, clip the plants over lightly with hedging clippers or sheep shears. This tidies and reshapes the plants, removing dead flowerheads.

Erica darleyensis 'Ghost Hills'

Erica carnea 'Springwood White'

Erica carnea 'White Perfection'

Erica carnea 'Myretoun Ruby'

Erica darleyensis
'Darley Dale'

Erica carnea
'Pink Mist'

Erica carnea 'Rosalie'

Left: *Winter-flowering heathers are available in shades of pink, mauve, purple and white. A few have golden foliage. All of them bring a splash of welcome color and interest to the garden.*

Above: *Erica carnea 'Pink Spangles', 'Springwood White' and 'Vivellii' make good ground cover. Plant them 9-10in(25cm) apart; they will cover the ground at the end of the first year.*

Heathers for summer flowers

Cultivars of *Calluna* (ling) and *Erica cinerea* provide continuity of color in a heather bed, as they flower mainly from mid- to late summer into the fall. Mix them with winter-flowering heathers and those with colored foliage to ensure a good year-round display in beds and borders with conifers. The plant labels will tell you exactly when different cultivars can be expected to flower, as this varies slightly from one type to another. Cultivars that flower well into fall look specially good under birches, where they make a dramatic contrast with the stark white bark of the trunks, and team well with deciduous plants displaying fall foliage tints. Use cultivars with a long flowering season to provide summer and fall color in a border of camellias and rhododendrons, which are spring-flowering. Acid-loving plants that flower at other times are specially valuable for out-of-season interest. Unlike winter heathers, the summer-flowering kind must grow in lime-free soil. If the soil is not naturally acid but merely neutral, you can improve it by adding moss peat, which is acidic. Sulfur chips are also available to acidify the soil - these last two years before another treatment is needed. (Avoid using powdered sulfur as it produces a very sudden change that does not last long.) Before using sulfur chips, however, you need to use a soil test kit to identify precisely what the acid-alkaline balance is so that you can assess the correct dosage.

Coping with chalky soils

It is not really practical to try and change chalky soil to make it suitable for ericaceous plants. In these conditions, it is better to grow summer heathers in tubs of ericaceous mix on a patio, or make a special raised bed for them. Fill this with ericaceous mix isolated from the soil beneath by a plastic sheet. Make sure that there is adequate drainage through the side walls of the bed. Use this for both summer and winter heathers, as well as conifers and acid-loving plants.

Calluna vulgaris 'Tib'

Calluna vulgaris 'Oxshott Common'

Calluna vulgaris 'Blazeaway'

Calluna vulgaris
'Fred Chapple'

Calluna vulgaris
'Silver Knight'

Calluna vulgaris
'Anne Marie'

Erica cinerea
'Contrast'

Erica cinerea
'Summer Gold'

Erica cinerea
'Sherry'

Calluna vulgaris
'Velvet Fascination'

Right: *A carpet of heathers densely planted in interlocking shapes makes a colorful picture all year round. The foliage of varieties not in flower act as a foil for those in bloom at any time.*

Summer and tree heathers

Summer-flowering heathers include a few kinds of *Erica*, such as *vagans*, and less common kinds, such as *Erica ciliaris* and *tetralix*, calluna (ling), tree heathers, such as *Erica arborea*, and *Daboecia*. When making a heather bed or using heathers as ground cover with conifers or shrubs, it pays to include as many different types as possible to create a rich, varied result, with an undulating effect. Although conifers or shrubs provide contrasts in size and shape, tree heathers are relatively rarely seen and worth hunting out, as they add feathery, spirelike shapes to a plant arrangement. They also team very well with a carpet of heathers. Remember that summer-flowering heathers need lime-free, or acid, soil. All heathers do best in well-drained soil in an open sunny situation, although a few individual varieties will tolerate some slight shade for part of the day. When planting a large area with heathers, plant groups of three or five of each variety for added impact. Space plants about 12in (30cm) apart so that they cover the ground within a year or so of planting. If you do not want to buy so many plants, start with one of each variety and take cuttings as shown. Heather cuttings root quickly and make plants big enough to set out after little more than a year. Take cuttings in late midsummer and keep them out of direct sunlight in an even temperature - a shady windowsill indoors is the best place. When they start to root after two or three months, make a few holes in the plastic covering the pot to start admitting air gradually. Extend the holes every week until, by the start of winter, you can remove the plastic entirely. Keep the pot on a cool windowsill indoors in better light or move it to a frost-free conservatory or greenhouse. Pot the cuttings individually in spring, using ericaceous compost with about 25% grit. From late spring onwards, stand them out on a bed of sand to keep the pots from drying out. Water and feed them regularly with a general liquid pot plant food and when the plants fill their pots, in late summer or fall, plant them out into the garden.

Above: *Stunning pink-purple drifts of Daboecia cantabrica 'Atropurpurea' make a deep carpet divided by thigh-deep paths between specimen conifers; an unusual idea for a larger garden.*

Left: Daboecia cantabrica 'Hookstone Pink'. *These plants are a type of summer-flowering heath, but grow larger than heathers, to about 18in (45cm) tall and 36in(90cm) or more in spread. The individual flowers are larger than those of heathers, but there are fewer of them on each spike. Few varieties are available; they all have purple, mauve, deep pink or white flowers. The foliage is heather-like but coarser and rather spiky, and dark green sometimes tinged bronzey according to variety. Provide them with sunny, well-drained, lime-free or acid conditions. Clip back the old foliage lightly in spring and topdress plants by sprinkling a peaty mulch between them at the same time.*

Right: Erica x veitchii 'Exeter' is the only hybrid tree heather regularly cultivated. It has bright green foliage and plumes of perfumed white flowers in spring. This medium sized plant is slightly tender in cold areas. Here it is planted with E. erigena 'Irish Salmon'.

Erica arborea 'Alpina' has dark green foliage. The summer flowers are white and bell-shaped, held towards the tips of the shoots and deliciously honey scented.

Tree heathers grow slowly to 5ft(1.5m) tall and about 2ft(60cm) across, with stems and foliage like large-scale heathers.

Erica arborea 'Albert's Gold' is valued for its pale gold foliage, which is brighter in summer. Tree heathers provide useful height and loose spire shapes in a heather bed. They prefer full sun, although they tolerate slight shade for part of the day.

Taking heather cuttings

The best time to propagate heathers is late midsummer. If you clip winter heathers after flowering, the new growth will be at the right stage for propagating by then; with summer-flowering varieties look for non-flowering shoots.

1 Take tip cuttings 1.5in(3.75cm) long from the current season's growth. Strip the tiny leaves from the lower half; take care not to bruise, skin or 'kink' the stems.

2 Dip the ends of the shoots into hormone rooting powder, using enough to cover the wounds where the leaves have been removed. Tap off any excess, then dibble in the cuttings using a small stick. Use a 50:50 blend of ericaceous mixture and silver sand to root the cuttings.

3 Water in gently and allow to drain. Cover the top of the pot with plastic film or a large plastic bag fixed around the sides of the pot. Leave this on for six to eight weeks.

A heather basket

The compact shape and free-flowering habit of winter-flowering heathers make them perfect for hanging baskets. Since they are well able to withstand the weather, you need not keep them in particularly sheltered situations, nor do the plants stop flowering or look battered if the weather turns nasty. In the Northern Hemisphere, there is no reason why you should not add ribbons, artificial berries, sprigs of holly, baubles or other decorations to give the container a festive touch for the Christmas period, or even illuminate it with colored outdoor fairy lights. The secret of success with any winter container is to buy evenly shaped plants just coming into flower at the start of the season and to fill it generously, as plants cannot be expected to grow and hide any gaps at that time of year.

3 *Knock the ivy out of its pot and plant it - with its stake - so that the top of the rootball is about 0.5in (1.25cm) below the rim of the pot. Firm gently so it stands up straight.*

4 *Tip out the two gold-leaved heathers and plant them close together at the front of the container, Their bright foliage complements the variegated markings in the ivy leaves.*

1 *Six heathers in small pots and a large variegated ivy with plenty of long trails are enough to fill a medium-sized hanging basket; this is a self-watering type for low maintenance.*

Three or five winter heathers make a good display on their own, but for more of a show add trailing variegated or frilly leaved ivy. Hang the finished basket sufficiently low so that you can see inside it.

2 *Roughly half-fill the basket with any good-quality potting mixture, but do not firm it down at this stage. If you are using a self-watering basket, do not fill the reservoir until you have finished planting up the basket.*

5 Use the flowering heathers to fill the sides of the basket, turning them so the shoots cascade over the edges to create the fullest possible display without swamping the smaller gold plants.

6 Using a small hand trowel, scoop a little extra potting mix into any gaps between the rootballs. This prevents the roots drying out, which could make the flowers finish early and cause the foliage to turn brown.

7 Cut the ties holding the ivy stems to the cane and untangle the 'trails' so they are all separate, ready to be arranged round the hanging basket.

Tying up the trails

Here, the trails are tied to the supporting chains. The effect is more dramatic, especially when the basket is to hang higher up and make a bold statement.

Right: Leave winter heathers in containers for one season only and then plant them in the garden in mid-spring.

8 Arrange the ivy trails around the edge of the basket and in the heather. This looks best where the inside of a low hanging basket will be easily visible.

A pot of winter heathers

Larger, low-level containers, such as windowboxes, tubs and troughs, allow for more expansive winter displays based around heathers. You can combine heathers with miniature conifers, small plants of evergreen shrubs, such as *Fatsia japonica* or variegated *Euonymus,* and evergreen grasses or alpines, and even tuck in temporary pots of flowering spring bulbs. If you use ericaceous potting mix, which winter heathers and conifers will not mind sharing, you can include lime-hating plants, such as *Skimmia* or *Gaultheria procumbens* for flowers or berries; both associate well with heathers. In mild city centers, nearly hardy indoor plants, such as winter cherry *(Solanum capsicastrum)* and Indian azalea *(Rhododendron simsii)*, could add a festive touch. Heathers can be difficult to team successfully with other plants, so stand plants together to test the effect of the group before buying. A fairly formal arrangement suits these types of plants best. In a large container, aim for a group of three upright evergreens of different heights with a carpet of heathers around it and other plants grouped amongst them. In a windowbox or trough, a row of identical evergreens or plants gently graduating to a central peak looks attractive.

1 *Team flowering heathers with a container in a matching color; go for frostproof ceramics. Even the conifer has reddish-purple stems and tinted foliage.*

4 *The conifer will form the centerpiece. Position it so that the top of the rootball is about 0.5in(1.25cm) below the rim of the container.*

2 *Cover the drainage hole with a 'crock' to contain the potting mix. Alternatively, use small gauge wire gauze, which also keeps out worms.*

3 *Fill one third of the container with potting mix. Ericaceous mix is not necessary, as winter heathers do not mind a little lime in their soil.*

6 *If the container is to stand against a wall, group the heathers more to the front and move the conifer closer to the back of the pot to make more room.*

5 *Firm the conifer down gently. Space the heathers evenly around it, squeezing the rootballs slightly to make them fit into the pot.*

Chamaecyparis thyoides 'Purple Heather'

7 *Fill the spaces between the heathers with extra potting mix until the container is loosely filled to just below the rim. This prevents the roots from drying out.*

Erica darleyensis 'Darley Dale'

Erica carnea 'March Seedling'

Erica carnea 'Rosalie'

Winter care

Site the container where it can be easily seen from the house. Although heathers and conifers are quite tough, stand the pot in a reasonably sheltered spot if it includes spring bulbs and alpines Do not assume that winter rains will take care of watering for you. Check the potting mix every week and water whenever it starts to feel dry just below the surface. In a windy spot, the potting mix will dry out faster so water more often. Feed in mild spells in spring with a general-purpose liquid feed or add slow-release fertilizer granules to containers when planting.

8 *Water thoroughly and sit the pot on a matching saucer in its final position to create a colorful display.*

A large heather display

Late summer and fall-flowering heathers in containers bridge the gap between summer bedding and the start of the winter-flowering heather season. Good examples include many varieties of *Calluna vulgaris* (ling) and *Erica vagans*. Both need acid conditions, so choose an ericaceous potting mix and team them with other lime-hating plants. Once the fall heathers are over, remove them, plant them out in the garden and put winter-flowering heathers into the same pot. (They will not mind the ericaceous mix.) Alternatively, a container like this could easily provide color and interest all year round, by substituting some of the late summer and fall heathers shown here for earlier flowering kinds, particularly those with colored foliage. They would then act as a permanent backdrop for the evergreens in the center of the display. The plants used here are a purple-leaved form of *Leucothoe* and a *Gaultheria* with lilac berries, although any acid-loving evergreens could be used. One good combination would be *Gaultheria procumbens*, a low creeper with deep green oval leaves and large bright red berries all winter, teamed with a dwarf rhododendron; the latter would flower in late spring, giving an even greater spread of seasonal interest.

1 *Cover the drainage hole with a crock, flat stone or 1in(2.5cm) of gravel. Part fill with ericaceous mix to just below the bottom planting pockets.*

2 *Buy heathers in small pots so that the rootballs will fit into the planting pockets. Tip the plants out of their pots and push them into the holes.*

3 *Add some more potting mixture to cover the roots and bring the level up to the next row of planting pockets. Add the remaining heathers.*

4 *Plant the top of the container. It is vital to fill up the pot, because plants put in towards the end of the season will not grow much more after planting.*

Leucothoe '*Carinella*'

Gaultheria mucronata

Calluna vulgaris '*Beoley Gold*'

Calluna vulgaris '*Alexandra*'

Calluna vulgaris '*Marleen*'

Calluna vulgaris '*Glencoe*'

Erica vagans '*Valerie Proudley*'

Calluna vulgaris '*Dark Beauty*'

Hedera helix '*Golden Ester*'

Calluna vulgaris '*Schurig's Sensation*'

Calluna vulgaris '*Alexandra*'

5 *Add two or three trailing ivies around the rim, pulling the trails through the handles and round between the heathers in the side pockets for an instantly mature finish.*

6 *Stand the pot in a sunny, sheltered spot and raise it up on 'pot feet' to aid drainage. Water it regularly and start feeding during the spring following planting with a liquid feed. As an all-year-round container, you could leave the pot undisturbed for two or three years before the plants grow too large and need replacing. Use this opportunity to replace the potting mix, too. Meantime, feed regularly with a liquid feed and water all year round.*

33

A festive winter arrangement

1 Assemble the ingredients; be sure to remove plants from their pots before planting them. Despite its name, 'Golden King', the standard holly is a female that bears red berries if there is a male holly nearby.

Evergreens form the basis of many pretty winter container arrangements, so why not consider making one specially with Christmas in mind? Festive foliage of holly and ivies forms the basis of this winter container display, backed up by traditional berries and evergreen foliage, plus an ornamental cabbage, which makes a long-lasting alternative to winter flowers. (Ornamental cabbages last until early spring, when they run to seed. They are not inhibited by bad weather, so you get a more reliable display.) If you cannot find a standard holly, you could use a poorly shaped bush and simply remove all but one of the stems to convert it into an instant standard. Alternatively, use a standard trained bay tree or a bushy holly with fewer surrounding plants. For a formal entrance, make a pair of matching pots and place one on either side of a porch. For a less formal look, team a single container with smaller but matching pots of evergreens, winter-flowering heathers and early spring bulbs. To keep winter displays looking their best, keep them in a well-sheltered spot, with containers raised up on pot feet out of puddles, and in as much light as possible. Even plants that normally prefer partial shade will thrive in better light during the dull winter days. Check containers regularly, even in winter, to see if they need watering; normal rainfall may not be able to get through the dense covering of foliage and into the potting mix. Feed during mild spells in spring. Pick off discolored leaves and generally tidy up container displays every week to keep them looking their best.

2 Cover the drainage hole with a crock or flat stone and part fill the pot with potting mixture, but leave enough room for the plant roots.

3 Stand the holly in the very center; add the golden tree heather at the base to soften the strong upright line of the trunk. Firm in gently.

4 Now add the Gaultheria and flowering heather to the front of the display, tucking potting mixture around their roots and firming them into place. Allow them to overflow the front of the pot.

5 Plant the taller ornamental cabbage in at the back of the display and add the trailing ivy, allowing the trails to curl round the sides of the pot towards the front. This gives an impression of instant maturity.

6 Stand the display on pot feet, say by a front door. Water well in and check weekly to make sure it does not dry out. No feeding will be needed until spring.

Ilex *x* altaclerensis 'Golden King'

Erica arborea 'Albert's Gold'

Gaultheria procumbens (checkerberry or partridge berry)

Ornamental cabbage

Hedera helix 'Sagittifolia' has long, narrow, arrowhead-shaped leaves,

Calluna vulgaris 'Alexandra'

35

A shallow bowl for winter

A shallow container makes a pleasant change from the usual pot-shaped types normally used for year-round plant displays, and teams well with more traditional types of arrangements to form an attractive group. The display shown here would, for instance, look very good teamed with the tall festive display featuring a standard holly tree as shown on page 34. Since shallow bowls dry out quickly, check them more often than usual to see if they need watering. And since they contain less potting mixture than a deeper container, they quickly become potbound (packed solid with roots) and the plants can become 'starved' of plant foods. Because of this, it makes sense to keep a potted display only for a single season before removing the plants and putting them out into the garden. When choosing plants to make up a winter arrangement, select those that are just coming up to their best, with flower buds beginning to open or foliage at its peak. Avoid small plants or those with obvious disease or damage. Completely fill the container, as the plants will not grow much more until the next growing season. Stand year-round containers of evergreens, heathers or conifers in a sunny but well-sheltered spot for the winter, raised up on pot feet to improve drainage. A site close to the house is best, since this is naturally sheltered by nearby walls, and in any case makes it easier to enjoy the containers without having to go outdoors.

Seasonal displays

Reasonably priced, ready-planted seasonal displays of small shrubs in containers are often available in garden centers. Enjoy them for the season and then plant them out in the garden. (This can be a cheap way of acquiring new plants.) Replant the container.

3 *Knock the plants out of their pots and sit the largest - here the Aucuba - in the center. Add smaller plants with contrasting shapes and leaf textures around the edge.*

1 *Choose a good-quality frost resistant bowl and cover the drainage hole with a crock or flat stone to stop the potting mix trickling out, whilst still allowing excess water to drain away.*

2 *Scoop enough potting mix into the container to roughly half-fill it, leaving plenty of room for the plant rootballs. Any good potting mixture will do, either soil- or peat-based.*

4 *Add a trailing plant (here we have used a Carex) to dangle over one side of the pot and center the Skimmia just in front of the Aucuba, as this will become the strongest attraction.*

Chamaecyparis lawsoniana 'Ellwood's Pillar'

Aucuba japonica 'Windsor Form'

Thuja orientalis 'Aurea Nana'

Skimmia reevesiana

Euonymus fortunei 'Blondie'

Calluna vulgaris 'Alexandra'

Erica vagans 'George Underwood'

Winter-flowering pansies

Carex oshimensis 'Evergold'

5 *Fill in any gaps around the edge of the pot, especially at the front, with flowering heathers. They will balance the effect of the red skimmia berries.*

6 *Reserve a space at the front for a handful of winter pansies. They will continue flowering through the winter. Deadhead them regularly.*

7 *Water the arrangement and stand it on a doorstep, by a porch or on the patio. Team it with other seasonal containers for greater effect.*

A sink garden

With their sculptured shapes and dense foliage, compact, slow-growing conifers make a good year-round backdrop for seasonal flowering rock plants, which enjoy the same growing conditions. A sink garden will need regular attention. Watering is the most frequent chore; you can't assume natural rainfall will be sufficient. Feed every two weeks from spring to late summer or add a slow-release fertilizer to the potting mix before planting the container, and add a new supply each spring by making a few holes in the potting mix and putting the feed down them. After two or three years the potting mix will be exhausted and need replacing, and some of the plants will have become untidy or overgrown, so the sink garden is best dismantled and remade using fresh plants. You can then plant out the old ones onto a rock garden or raised bed.

2 *Cover the large drainage holes in the bottom of the container with flat pieces of stone or broken pieces of clay flowerpot. Add a 1in(2.5cm) layer of coarse gravel to cover the base of the container evenly.*

3 *Now part fill the 'sink' with soil-based potting mixture, leaving enough room to take the plants when standing in their pots, plus a margin of about 0.5in (1.25cm) between the pot and the rim of the container.*

1 *Choose a mixture of plants that contrast well together in shape, texture and color while providing year-round interest. You will also need a bag of soil-based potting mixture.*

4 *Carefully position the largest plants; they will make the most impact on the finished arrangement. Knock the plants out of their pots and stand them in place; position a curving conifer so it leans towards the center of the container.*

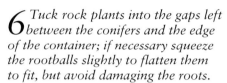

5 Place the second conifer alongside and push both conifers as close to the back of the container as possible, since they will be the tallest plants and will form a background to the display.

6 Tuck rock plants into the gaps left between the conifers and the edge of the container; if necessary squeeze the rootballs slightly to flatten them to fit, but avoid damaging the roots.

7 Plants with a slightly trailing habit at the front of the container will cascade over the edge and soften the hard lines. Use plenty of plants so that the container looks full.

8 Add a little extra potting mix to fill any gaps between rootballs. After watering in, this extra mix will probably sink slightly, so top up any depressions with extra mixture later.

Hedera helix 'Conglomerata'

Chamaecyparis pisifera 'Nana Aureovariegata'

Sempervivum 'Pruhonice'

Chamaecyparis pisifera 'Golden Nymph'

Sedum lydium

Arabis fernandii 'Coburgii Variegata'

Thymus 'Doone Valley'

Hypericum empetrifolium prostratum

Planting up a group of conifers

Conifers make good plants for all-year-round displays. Smaller or less dramatic conifers look best placed together in a group of five small or three medium-sized plants. Choose plants with distinctively different shapes - one neat and domed, one irregular and bushy, and one tall and spreading, as here, make a good trio. And make the most of the shelter on, say, a patio to grow choice conifers that need some protection or slow-growing kinds that may be difficult to accommodate in the garden. Choose the same style containers for the whole group to 'link' them together visually. Terracotta, oriental ceramic and natural-look wood or stone containers go specially well with conifers. The containers look best if, like the plants, they are all of different sizes. Put the largest plant in the biggest container to keep the plants and pots in scale with each other. The containers need not all be the same shape; one might be wide and shallow and the others tall and upright. A wide, shallow container would suit a low spreading conifer very well.

Right: *Assemble a 'nest' of three matching pots in different sizes, potting mixture and three conifer plants chosen to look good together as a group. Assess the effect of different plant combinations in the garden center before making a final choice.*

1 Tackle one pot at a time; cover the drainage hole in the bottom with a piece of curved broken clay flower pot. This stops the potting mixture from trickling out but allows surplus water to run away.

2 Part fill the pot with any good-quality potting mixture - soil-based kinds are best since the plants will remain in their pots for several years. Leave room for the rootball, plus about 0.5in (1.25cm).

Watering and feeding plants

Water-retaining gel crystals added to the potting mix help to hold water. Consider installing an automatic drip-watering system linked to an outdoor tap via a water computer that is set to switch the water on for a particular time every day. Hide feeder pipes behind pots, trellis or even under paving slabs. Use liquid or soluble feeds every week during spring and summer or add slow-release feed granules or sticks when planting up pots. Plants can remain in the same mix for up to three years. If they become too big, transfer them into larger containers after this time or plant them in the garden.

Picea orientalis *'Aurea'*. This gold version of the oriental spruce looks its best in the spring, when the new young shoots are cream colored. They are bright gold during the summer, finally becoming green with age.

3 Knock each plant carefully out of its pot and sit it in the center of the container. If it is potbound, tease a few roots out from the rootball.

4 Trowel more potting mix around the rootball and firm down gently, leaving a gap of about 0.5in(1.25cm) below the rim for watering.

5 Water well in. If the potting mix sinks after watering, top up to the original level and water again. Allow surplus water to drain away.

Cryptomeria japonica *'Lobbii Nana'* is a dense, compact, craggy shaped plant that reaches less than 2ft(60cm) in any direction after 10 years.

Thuja plicata *'Rogersii'* reaches just 12in(30cm) in any direction after ten years. The outer tips of the shoots are golden-bronze.

6 Pot all three plants in the same way and then group them together attractively on a patio or similar vantage point, where they can be seen against a plain background that accentuates their dramatic shapes.

A selection of conifers

Conifers are so called because they bear cones as their seed-carrying devices; the flowers are mainly insignificant. In some conifers, such as pines, the male flowers develop as 'candles'; in some others, the male flowers are tiny red 'blobs'. It is the female 'flowers' that develop into cones, with the seeds held tightly between the scales to protect them from birds. When the cone is ripe, the scales open out to allow the seed to fall away. Most conifers are evergreen, although a few species do shed their leaves in winter. This brief overview of conifers from *Abies* to *Thuja* introduces the variety of conifers featured in the rest of the book.

ABIES
Nowadays, a good selection of compact varieties of Abies (silver fir) exist suitable for gardens. Some varieties are cultivated for their attractive cones.

Abies lasiocarpa 'Compacta', very slow growing, with blue-gray foliage and even, conical shape. Use in a border with low, ground-covering plants or in a patio pot. Reaches 3ft (90cm) in ten years.

CEDRUS
While none of the cedars are very small, some kinds are suitable for medium to large gardens, where their striking shapes give character to a lawn or large border.

Cedrus deodara 'Aurea'. An exceptionally striking medium to large specimen conifer with a nodding tip and gold-tinged foliage, especially conspicuous in spring when new growth appears. Reaches about 8ft(2.5m) in ten years.

CHAMAECYPARIS
There are probably more kinds of Chamaecyparis (false cypress) for growing in gardens than any other kind of conifer; the range is immense and includes large plants suitable for lawn specimens or large hedges, through to the tiniest rock garden gems. All need a sheltered site to protect the foliage.

Chamaecyparis lawsoniana 'Little Spire' forms an irregular craggy spire, illuminated with masses of tiny red male flowers ('cones') in spring - a feature of the variety. Expect it to reach about 6ft(2m) in ten years. Good for rock gardens, pots and raised beds and in well-drained borders of dwarf conifers and grasses or small herbaceous plants.

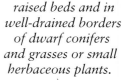

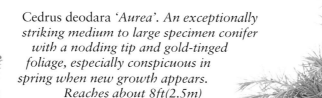

Left: *Conifers need not be grown together or with heathers; those with striking foliage and/or good color associate well with other garden plants. Here, Chamaecyparis pisifera 'Filifera Aurea' grows with euonymus, various colored ornamental sages, mahonia and golden yew.*

Chamaecyparis nootkatensis *'Pendula'* is an upright-growing conifer with pronounced weeping foliage; on a well-grown specimen, this resembles layers of overlapping fringes. Makes an upright-conical shape, reaching almost 10ft(3m) in ten years. Grow as a specimen plant surrounded by grass or in a large bed with low, ground-covering plants, such as heathers.

Chamaecyparis lawsoniana *'Snow White'*. The white-tipped young shoots give it a piebald appearance. Grow with dark green varieties, horizontal conifers or low, ground cover plants for contrast. Develops into a roughly conical plant 3ft (90cm) tall in ten years.

CRYPTOMERIA

Japanese cedars (Cryptomeria) make large trees, but cultivars are much more compact, while some are positive miniatures suitable for the rockery. In many cultivars, the feathery looking foliage takes on deep bronze-red tones in the fall.

Above: Cryptomeria japonica *'Elegans Nana' is a compact form of the Japanese cedar with feathery foliage that turns a rich plum-crimson in winter.*

Cryptomeria japonica *'Elegans Compacta'. This compact form has soft feathery foliage that grows in tiers at first, becoming denser with age and turning bronze-red in winter. All cryptomerias prefer rather moister soil than most conifers. This one grows slowly to make a mound-shaped plant 3ft(90cm) high in ten years.*

Left: *Here, a pair of tall, cylindrical Cupressus macrocarpa 'Goldcrest' have been tied together at the top to form an unusual all-year-round archway, strategically planted to frame a view down the garden.*

CUPRESSUS

Cypresses are typically tall, upright-conical trees with soft foliage. Cupressus macrocarpa was once popular for hedging, but cypresses are now mainly used as specimen trees in medium-to-large gardens.

The striking Cupressus glabra 'Aurea' teams specially well with dark green and blue heathers or deep green evergreens and berrying plants. It reaches about 8ft (2.5m) in 10 years.

Above: Juniperus communis 'Golden Showers' is a gold-leaved form of the rockery species. It makes a pretty flame-shaped, small to medium plant.

Right: Juniperus squamata 'Blue Carpet' is ideal for cracks between paving, path edges, and for ground cover in a hot, sunny, 'difficult' spot.

In spring, the new growth at the shoot tips of Juniperus communis 'Depressa Aurea' is butter yellow; during summer, the silvery undersides of the leaves make bright highlights amongst the foliage, and in winter, the color takes on strong bronzey hues.

JUNIPERS
Junipers are tough, rugged conifers that tolerate hot dry situations without turning brown. This makes them ideal for patios, in gravel or in pots. The foliage is hard and spiky, so site plants with care.

The steely blue foliage of Juniperus virginiana 'Blue Arrow' holds its color well all year round and its strong shape is useful for creating a contrast with other distinctively shaped plants in a small group, perhaps on a patio, or in a heather and conifer bed.

PICEA

Picea, commonly known as spruce, are available in a wide range of garden cultivars, with blue, silver, gray or green foliage growing in a variety of shapes. Many have attractive cones that hang down below the branches.

Picea pungens *'Erich Frahm'* is a slow-growing, compact, broadly conical-shaped blue spruce, good as a specimen plant in a small border, but also fine in a pot on the patio.

Picea glauca *'Laurin'* grows to perhaps 12in (30cm) high in ten years. It makes a wonderful dense habit and neat shape, ideal for pots or in rock gardens or raised beds.

Right: The remains of male flowers, called candles, with young female cones and mature cones of Scots pine (Pinus sylvestris). The cones of this conifer take two years to ripen before opening out their scales to release the seeds from deep within the cone.

Above: *Prostrate forms of blue spruce, such as this* Picea pungens *'Glauca Prostrata', may produce upright-growing shoots; prune them out at once or the plant tends to revert to a more upright growth habit.*

PINUS

Pines have small bundles of needles for foliage, which can often be quite long and form a feature of the plant. Plants quickly develop a rugged appearance, which lends maturity to the garden. Large cones are a feature of some varieties.

Pinus sylvestris *'Chantry Blue'* has stunning silvery blue foliage and orange 'candles' on young growth in spring. A rugged plant that tolerates fairly poor or dry conditions and exposure to wind, but needs plenty of sun.

TAXUS

Yew, the traditional plant for formal hedging and topiary work, has been used in country gardens for centuries; it once supplied the wood for longbows. Its reputation for being slow growing is not entirely deserved; young plants fill out to form a serviceable hedge faster than is generally supposed.

Left: *Yew is probably the most amenable conifer for close clipping, hence its popularity for hedging and topiary work. Solid shapes, such as hedges and topiary spheres, and boxes, as here, are self-supporting, but fancier shapes need an interior framework of metal rods for support.*

Thuja orientalis 'Aurea Nana' is an immensely popular conifer, grown for many years as a rockery plant or in small conifer borders. The overlapping flattened fans of gold foliage (brightest in spring) are characteristic of the variety. Makes a neat rounded plant reaching about 2ft(60cm) tall in ten years.

Thuja occidentalis 'Rheingold' makes a loose-conical shape and reaches 4ft(1.2m) in ten years. Use it as a feature plant for a large rock garden, in mixed heather and conifer borders or even planted in a single row as an unusual non-clip informal hedge.

THUJA

Thujas have flattened sprays of soft foliage, scented in some species, formed by rows of overlapping scales. There are some good hedging species, but ornamental cultivars of thuja are decorative in borders.

Taxus baccata 'Fastigiata Aureomarginata' looks specially good by a doorway. It reaches 6ft(2m) in ten years. Can be clipped if necessary.

Collecting small conifers

The bright gold-tipped foliage of Taxus baccata 'Pumila Aurea' persists well even in winter. Plenty of sun is essential to keep a good color.

Conifers are very compulsive; once you have a few interesting plants in a range of shapes, colors and textures, you want to collect more. Start with small conifers, as they are simple to house without dramatically affecting the look of the garden. A collection of compact, slow-growing plants looks good in pots; standing them on a patio is an increasingly popular way of displaying conifers and one that makes for a very low-maintenance display, since you do not need to replant in spring and fall, as with annuals. Really small conifers can be grown on shelves, tiered staging or the type of raised plinths used to display bonsai collections. (Dwarf conifers in pots are as good as bonsai, but do not need any trimming and training, as each variety will naturally grow into its own characteristic shape.) Conifers in pots need regular watering, especially in summer and if the pots are small; if they dry out, the foliage turns brown and never really recovers. An automatic 'drip' watering system, with a separate nozzle for each pot, is worth considering unless you have plenty of time for watering. Provide a sheltered, sunny spot, in free-draining soil, and feed potted conifers all through the growing season with a good-quality liquid feed containing trace elements.

Chamaecyparis obtusa 'Nana Compacta' is an ultra mini cultivar with a dense curly growth habit. It reaches less than 2ft(60cm) in ten years.

Pinus wallichiana *'Densa' is a rare conifer with very dense foliage that makes a compact conical shape reaching 3ft(90cm) in ten years.*

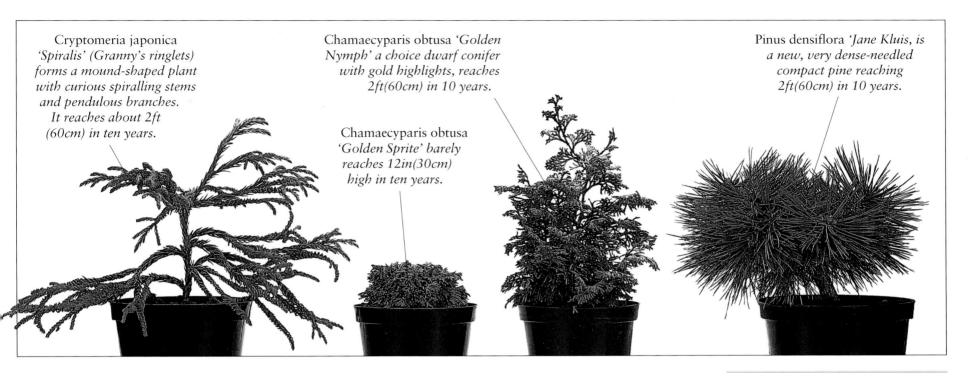

Cryptomeria japonica 'Spiralis' (Granny's ringlets) forms a mound-shaped plant with curious spiralling stems and pendulous branches. It reaches about 2ft (60cm) in ten years.

Chamaecyparis obtusa 'Golden Nymph' a choice dwarf conifer with gold highlights, reaches 2ft(60cm) in 10 years.

Chamaecyparis obtusa 'Golden Sprite' barely reaches 12in(30cm) high in ten years.

Pinus densiflora 'Jane Kluis, is a new, very dense-needled compact pine reaching 2ft(60cm) in 10 years.

Chamaecyparis obtusa 'Nana Aurea' has an open habit and slowly grows into a loose conical shape, reaching 3ft(90cm) in ten years.

Thujopsis dolabrata 'Nana' makes a compact, flat-topped, bushy shape, reaching 18in(45cm) high and about 48in(120cm) across after ten years.

Dwarf conifers in raised beds

Another alternative is to grow a collection of dwarf conifers in raised beds, an alpine sink or a trough garden. Use a mixture of good-quality topsoil and gritty sand and plant them with rock plants - avoid teaming very dwarf conifers with heathers, as after a few years the heathers will smother them.

Chamaecyparis pisifera 'Nana Aureovariegata' is very compact and slow growing and can grow to about 8x12ft(2.5x3.7m) after ten years.

Larger collectable conifers

As well as the popular range of conifers available in garden centers, there are also many choice, uncommon kinds that are well worth hunting for. Look for them in nurseries that specialize in conifers or trace them via specialist horticultural societies and publications devoted to sourcing unusual plants. Enthusiasts who specialize in any particular kind of plant often use their collection to form the basis of an area of the garden or perhaps even the entire garden. Larger conifers can be planted in grass arboretum-style (the proper name for a collection of conifers grown this way is a pinetum) or used as background planting in mixed borders with more modest-sized conifers, along with heathers and grasses, etc. With scarce or valuable plants, it is always worth taking particular pains over cultivation, since such plants are difficult - sometimes impossible - to replace. Prepare the soil very well before planting and stake upright varieties for the first few years to ensure that they maintain the correct shape. Keep new plants well watered and mulch them every spring to keep the roots moist and prevent lower branches turning brown. It is also advisable to feed a conifer collection with a special conifer fertilizer, ideally one containing fish meal or seaweed (for trace elements), so that the foliage color develops fully.

Abies koreana *'Silberlocke'*, a distinctive form of the popular Korean fir, has silvery backs to the leaves that curl upwards, giving an interesting two-tone effect. It reaches about 5ft(1.5m) in ten years.

Chamaecyparis lawsoniana *'Wissels Saguaro'* is a rare new columnar conifer with tightly packed foliage and an irregular outline suggestive of the saguaro cactus. Grows to about 5ft(1.5m) in ten years.

Left: Cryptomeria japonica 'Cristata' makes a conical bush about 10ft (3m) in ten years. It occasionally produces flattened tips to some shoots, which develop into green crests much fancied by flower arrangers. Needs good soil, shelter and plenty of sun.

Left: Cedrus libani 'Sargentii' is a dual-purpose conifer. If trained up a stake, it develops into a graceful weeping tree; if allowed to run along the ground, it grows as ground cover. Provide sun and good-quality soil.

Sequoiadendron giganteum 'Glaucum' is a rare, narrow- shaped conifer with distinctive blue-gray whipcord foliage. Given good drainage and sun, it can reach 12ft(3.7m) in 10 years.

Pinus *x* schwerinii *is a rare variety grown for its long, elegant drooping needles. It grows to 15ft(4.5m) in 10 years.*

Sciadopitys verticillata *(Japanese umbrella pine) has long needles radiating outwards. This slow starter stays dwarf for ten years but eventually makes a big tree.*

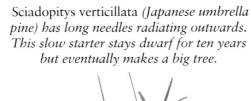

51

Silver firs

Mention *Abies* (silver fir) and most people think of forests full of huge commercial conifers. But the family also contains some very choice, decorative, small- and medium-sized plants for the garden. Many are of the traditional Christmas tree shape - upright-conical, with branches arranged in tiers - but there are also smaller, chunkier shapes with dense bushy foliage. The gems of the family are the really dwarf kinds and the Korean fir, which are very garden worthy. Most abies look their best as young specimens; as they age, the upright-growing kinds particularly tend to lose their bottom branches - a perfectly natural occurrence. (It can even be an advantage, as it allows more light and air through and creates extra planting space underneath.) Prostrate and bushy miniature kinds, however, behave just like any other dwarf conifer and remain fully clad. Large and medium-growing *Abies* cultivars make good trees for planting in woodland, as they are naturally at home in a forest situation. They associate well with both other conifers and deciduous trees, and look specially stunning mixed with trees that color up well in the fall, such as acers. Smaller, choice kinds make good plants for borders, including heather beds. Some kinds, particularly the Korean fir *(Abies koreana)* are notable for their striking cones. These stand up from the branch (unlike many conifers where they are lost amongst the foliage) and are produced on very young plants; most conifers do not start bearing cones until they are many years old. In *Abies koreana,* the young cones are violet, often with what looks like wax (actually resin) dripping down them. This feature makes the plant specially valuable for small gardens. Abies enjoy a deep moist soil tending towards acid, but tolerate most kinds except shallow or very chalky soils and those that dry out badly in summer.

Above: One of the real pygmies of the family, Abies balsamea 'Nana', makes a neat ball of curly foliage with bright green tips when the new growth appears in early summer. Naturally neat, it stays under 12in(30cm) across in 10 years - ideal for a rockery that does not dry out severely.

Abies balsamea hudsonia. *A dwarf slow-growing form of balsam fir, with a very dense growth habit and rather flattened top.*

Left: Abies koreana 'Silberlocke' is an improved form of the Korean fir (which can look a bit leggy when young). It combines violet cones with silvery backed foliage and dense compact growth - a most attractive combination.

Abies koreana 'Silberlocke'. This is the silver version of the well-known Korean fir. Most of the silvering is on the underside of the leaves, giving the plant an interesting two-tone appearance.

Below: Abies concolor 'Glauca Compacta' makes an irregular bushy shape with silvery blue-tinged foliage, which is at its best in early summer, since it is the new growth that is most strongly colored. This slow-growing and naturally tiny variety reaches 36in(90cm) in ten years, but rarely attains more than 6-8ft(2-2.5m) when fully grown.

Graceful cedars

Cedars are easy-to-grow conifers that naturally make striking shapes. Most of the well-known kinds, such as *Cedrus atlantica* 'Glauca' and *C. deodara* 'Aurea', eventually grow into large imposing trees, ideal as specimens surrounded by lawn or a low carpet of ground cover plants. *C. a.* 'Glauca Pendula', a stunning pendulous form, is sometimes trained over pergola poles or over handrails down the side of garden steps. The blue trailing foliage makes a most unusual and attractive 'living screen'. Grown as a free-standing tree, it forms a graceful weeping specimen that is wider than it is tall. A few compact cultivars of *Cedrus* are suitable for rock gardens, though these are not widely available in garden centers. Cedars enjoy a reasonably well-drained soil, but will tolerate clay as long as it has been improved with grit and organic matter to provide some aeration and drainage. Give them shelter from the strongest winds; in exposed areas, young plants especially can shed many of their needles, resulting in a rather balding appearance until new growth appears. One of the main attractions of cedars is the brilliant coloration of the new growth in spring. Bluish-gray or blue-green cultivars appear to be highlighted with pale blue, while goldish cultivars have bright gold tips to the shoots that give the whole plant a variegated look. The shade cast by pyramidal varieties is too deep for anything to grow directly under a tree after more than a few years and the lower branches trail on the ground. By then quite a heavy fall of old needles will have built up under the tree. These act as a mulch and this plus the shade mean that weeds rarely live under cedars.

Right: The young spring growth of C. deodara *introduces fresh green highlights into the foliage. The golden form 'Aurea' is smaller and slower, more suited to medium sized-gardens.*

C. deodora 'Golden Horizon' is one of the few cedars that makes a bushy plant.

Right: *Mature specimens of* Cedrus atlantica *'Glauca' produce a profusion of medium-sized cones that stand upright out of the dense foliage and provide additional seasonal interest.*

Left: *Cedrus atlantica 'Glauca', a traditional favorite, makes a large, shapely, blue-green tree with distinctive upward- and outward-growing branches.*

If you want to train C. a. 'Glauca Pendula' over pergola poles or arches, take care to train the trunk up a stout stake for the first few years, or the plant will simply flop and sprawl on the ground.

Medium-sized chamaecyparis

If you are looking for specimen plants, then some of the more striking medium-sized chamaecyparis are ideal. Choose plants with character - good or even architectural shapes - that will make an impact when planted on their own or in small groups in grass, in a bed of heather, or as prostrate ground cover, or on either side of a doorway. For average gardens, it is also worth choosing cultivars that are fairly slow growing and do not grow too big, so that they stay in proportion to their surroundings. These types of chamaecyparis like reasonable soil, but do not need the very special conditions required by miniature rock garden types. A sunny situation is important, however, otherwise growth becomes soft and and straggly instead of tight and crisp, and colored conifers fail to develop their proper hue. Occasional feeds with liquid seaweed in spring and early summer help color to develop, even in a good sunny site. Plants that naturally grow into a distinctive shape make the best specimen plants. Look for neat, upright pillar shapes, such as *C. lawsoniana* 'Green Pillar' and the deeper green, splay-topped 'Ellwoodii', to make a formal statement. More curious are the eccentrically shaped spires of *C. l.* 'Little Spire' or *C. obtusa* 'Tetragona Aurea', perfect for highlighting a planted carpet. For dramatic impact try the weeping stems of *C. nootkatensis* 'Pendula'. But where a more geometric cone- or flame-shaped plant is needed, go for the neat, powder blue cone shape of *C. l.* 'Stewartii' or one of the many medium-sized, bright golden cultivars of *C. lawsoniana*. Arguably the one that keeps its color best in winter is *C. l.* 'Lanei'. However, a good conifer specialist is likely to stock a wide range of the less well-known cultivars for you to choose from.

C. lawsoniana 'Columnaris Glauca', a blue-green foliage form, retains a neat shape with a pointed top. Grows to 8-10 ft (2.5-3m) high and 3ft(90cm) across in ten years.

Right: *The gold filigree foliage of C. pisifera 'Golden Mop' creates a very eye-catching centerpiece in a garden of conifers, evergreens and fall foliage color. Give it a sunny spot.*

Chamaecyparis pisifera 'Filifera Nana' has green foliage and grows very slowly to make a small- to medium-sized dome-shaped bush with a flat top. The yellow form 'Filifera Aurea' looks like a small pile of bright golden whipcord. The green form, 'Filifera', grows rather faster, but has the same hempen texture.

Right: Although sold as a dwarf conifer, Chamaecyparis obtusa 'Tetragona Aurea' is merely a slow starter. From 3ft(90cm) high at 10 years, it can eventually reach 12-15ft (3.7-4.5m), though large specimens are rarely seen. The foliage has a wonderful chunky feathery texture, but may brown at the ends if grown in a windy spot.

Chamaecyparis 'Ellwood's Gold' has unique, lacy, gold-edged foliage.

Above: The gold of C. lawsoniana 'Lanei' does not fade in winter. It is strongest at the shoot tips, which contrast with the darker green interior of the tree. The effect is almost lacy.

Below: The flare-topped flame shape and rich green lacy foliage of C. l. 'Ellwoodii' team specially well with modern buildings, heather beds and stonework. It is a plant with real character.

Compact chamaecyparis

Plenty of dwarf conifers are sold as suitable for growing in rockeries and pots, and few are more popular than the compact chamaecyparis. The reasons are not hard to find; their tight lacy foliage, almost imperceptibly slow growth and delightful dwarf shapes make them more like growing pets than plants. However, to do well they need reasonable soil with adequate nutrients, one that holds moisture but drains freely and never dries right out in summer. Bear in mind that the sort of plants you grow with chamaecyparis must also tolerate more moisture and not be very drought-tolerant kinds. Gentians, raymondas, mossy saxifrages, alpine violas and dwarf campanulas, pulsatilla and alpine phlox are all good choices. Avoid sprawling rock plants that may smother small conifers, as heavy shade makes the foliage turn brown. Also avoid dwarf spring bulbs, such as species tulips, as these must have very dry conditions when dormant in summer, or they rot. In rock gardens, you should add plenty of well-rotted organic matter to the planting hole for dwarf chamaecyparis. They need regular watering for the first season until they are properly established; from then on, watering is only necessary in dry spells. In pots, give dwarf chamaecyparis any good potting mixture - a soil-based kind is best, as you can then leave them for several years without repotting. However, it is a good idea to replace the top 1in(2.5cm) of potting mix each spring. Keep the plants well watered and feed them regularly during the growing season (late spring to late summer) with a good, general-purpose feed containing trace elements - or feed seaweed extract separately; this is specially valuable for maintaining the intensity of colored forms.

Above: Distinctive architectural shapes look good emerging from a carpet of heathers. This 'bun' is a well-grown Chamaecyparis lawsoniana 'Minima'.

C. lawsoniana 'Minima Aurea' is slow growing, with tightly packed, rather curly looking gold foliage that contrasts well with the deep green center of the bush. It remains a good gold color all year round.

C. thyoides 'Andelyensis' forms a very dense, almost tubular plant, with flames of foliage at the top.

Conifer flowers

Chamaecyparis lawsoniana 'Little Spire' makes a craggy spire shape, which in spring produces a brilliant display of bright red male flowers. Grows to about 4ft(1.2m) in ten years.

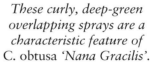

Above: C. pisifera 'Nana' grows into a real mini-mound and makes an ideal accompaniment for choice rock plants with equally modest habits.

Compact chamaecyparis

Above: C. obtusa 'Nana Gracilis' is one of the most easily recognized and popular compact conifers - in fact, the perfect rock gardener's pet.

C. obtusa 'Nana Lutea' closely resembles C. obtusa 'Nana Gracilis', except that it is bright gold. It holds its color well in winter.

C. pisifera 'Nana' has soft, almost permed foliage and develops a perfect cushion shape.

These curly, deep-green overlapping sprays are a characteristic feature of C. obtusa 'Nana Gracilis'.

59

An instant 'bonsai' conifer

Some conifers are traditional subjects for bonsai, notably Japanese white pine, larch and mountain pine, though junipers, cryptomeria, cedars and others are sometimes used. These are coaxed to resemble ancient and stunted trees by a combination of trimming, wiring and root pruning over many years. 'Proper' bonsai requires a great deal of knowledge, care and attention, but with a little trimming, it is possible to accentuate the natural characteristics of virtually any conifer or create interesting shapes of your own. Naturally dwarf types that can be grown in pots are the most convenient to work on, but you can also trim larger conifers growing in the open garden. (However, if you make a mess of it, the result cannot be kept out of sight until the effect of the bad haircut 'grows out'.) To start with, find a plant that is already growing into an interesting shape - perhaps a lopsided specimen at a garden center or one of the varieties that typically grows into an uneven shape. Trimming can mean thinning out cluttered growth to reveal the true shape of the plant, or altering the entire shape of the plant. Very dense-packed conifers with tiny leaves, such as some of the chamaecyparis, can also be given topiary shapes - domes, spirals or peacock shapes - small-scale versions of the type of trimming done using the traditional yew. However, for a reasonable-looking result do not stray too far from the basic framework shape of the plant, and try to finish up with a plant whose 'visual' weight is evenly balanced from one side of the trunk to the other.

Chamaecyparis obtusa 'Nana Gracilis', a compact cultivar, ideal for trimming and shaping. Think carefully before you cut; dwarf conifers are very slow and mistakes take a long time to grow out.

1 Choose a frost-proof terracotta pot of oriental design to underline the bonsai feel. Cover the drainage hole with a flat stone or crock and part fill with soil-based potting mix.

2 Select a naturally 'craggy' plant, knock it out of its pot and plant it in the center of the container. It need not be upright - sometimes a slight lean accentuates a natural feature.

3 Water the plant well in to settle the potting mixture around the roots. If the mixture sinks badly, simply fill in with a little extra mix and rewater as before.

4 Look closely at the natural shape of the plant and plan what you want to alter before cutting. Use sharp scissors, secateurs or bonsai trimming shears, and do a little at a time.

The majority of conifers put on most of their year's growth in one big spurt in late spring, so this is the time to retrim every year to keep the shape neat. Nip off odd out of place sprigs at any time.

5 Clip away small sections of foliage to accentuate that part of the shape you want to exaggerate. Stop, stand back and look at the result after removing each piece to see the effect.

6 To help you decide whether to remove a section of foliage or not, try 'blanking' it out with a piece of card. This is much better than cutting it off and then wishing you hadn't!

7 The shape emerges little by little. Take your time; meditation is all part of the art. The shape of this plant looks rather like a peacock - it could easily end up as one.

8 Continue thinning out until you are happy with what is left. Avoid getting carried away; it is easy enough to take off a bit more later, but it takes ages to grow new foliage into a gap.

9 The finished plant retains the attractive lacy texture and billowing shape of the original, but now it can all be seen more clearly.

Globular and bushy chamaecyparis

Below: C. l. 'Green Globe' is one of the smallest of the family, making a neat, 'pudding basin' shape. Snip off any wayward strands to keep the shape in perfect condition.

In more informal situations, such as a large walk-through rock garden, a small bed or border, or a conifer collection where a range of shapes is important, a bushier, compact, 'character' conifer may be called for. *Chamaecyparis pisifera* 'Boulevard' is a good choice with strong upright and prostrate shapes, while another real head-turner is *C. p.* 'Filifera Aurea'. Plant it with chunky pine trunks, bamboos, or deep blue or green foliage for best effect, though while young it makes a good specimen for a pot on the patio. Another stunner is *C. thyoides* 'Rubicon'; its wine red stems are clearly visible through misty-mauve-tinted juniperlike foliage, which deepens to a subtle shade approaching pewter in winter. Globular chamaecyparis are very popular now, especially the ultracompact kinds, such as *C. lawsoniana* 'Green Globe', used for rockeries. Variegated kinds are more unusual; *C. pisifera* 'Squarrosa Sulphurea', has feathery sulfur-yellow foliage, fading to light khaki in winter. For a sophisticated look, team it with toning shades - say purple or mauve flowers with the purplish *C. thyoides* 'Rubicon'. For a complete contrast use 'opposite' colors, such as bright red rhodohypoxis with moss green *C. l.* 'Green Globe'. Plant 'character' chamaecyparis in soil that does not dry out badly in summer, and avoid planting them with neighbors that may smother or shade them, which will ruin their characteristic shapes and colors.

Left: C. thyoides *cultivars have a natural purplish-gray tinge to the foliage, which is most strongly pronounced in the unusual cultivar 'Heather Bun'; it looks wonderful teamed with a carpet of heathers.*

Below: *Slow-growing* C. pisifera *'Sungold' resembles a heap of golden whipcord. Team it with interesting barks, such as pine, birch or dogwood.*

When buying conifers, such as this C. p. 'Boulevard', choose plants with bright, fresh healthy looking foliage.

Dull, dried out plants may not have been kept watered and will take time to recover - if they ever do.

Below: Gold-tinged conifers with distinctive shapes add color and variety all year round. This is C. l. 'Pygmaea Argentea', a compact cultivar that reaches 12in(30cm) high in 10 years.

Right: C. pisifera 'Boulevard' has soft, tufted, blue-green foliage with turquoise highlights and a conical cumulus cloud shape. It is one of the few conifers that is easily rooted from cuttings.

Cryptomerias

Japanese cedars (*Cryptomeria japonica* and its cultivars) originated from Japan and China, and many forms grow naturally into shapes vaguely reminiscent of pagodas. This makes them good additions to oriental-style gardens, where they associate well with dwarf pines, Japanese maples and a carpet of cobblestones or raked sand. However, they team well with most conifers and also evergreen shrubs, since their unusual shapes or dense-packed textures, often combined with foxy red or bronze highlights or fall coloration, provide strong contrasts with their neighbors. Reddish or bronze-tinged cultivars 'go' especially well with heathers, too; the soft, feathery foliage of cryptomerias specially complements that of heathers. When grouped with deep red-flowered heathers and those with red, orange or gold foliage, they make very good plant associations. Cryptomeria likes the same conditions as most heathers - acid soil and lots of sun - so the two are naturally perfect partners. The most popular species is *Cryptomeria japonica* 'Elegans', which makes a beautiful, upright specimen 6ft(2m) tall in ten years, whose branches are at first arranged in tiers rather like a wedding cake, but later 'fill in' with dense packed foliage. However, most of the other cultivars remain much smaller and some are compact enough to use on rock gardens and raised beds. Since the plants dislike dry soil, be sure to add plenty of well-rotted organic matter before planting. And unless you are very sure of your watering, they are not good subjects to grow in pots; they only need to dry out badly once to be dead. Even when planted in the soil, browning foliage and 'hard' stunted growth is a common problem if conditions are not adequately moist. However do not overcompensate by planting them in a waterlogged spot, which is almost as bad.

Cryptomeria japonica *'Bandai-Sugi', a very close-textured, dwarf and slow-growing cultivar, becomes rather irregularly shaped with age.*

Cryptomeria japonica *'Globosa Nana' makes a flattish dome shape.*

Left: Cryptomeria japonica *'Globosa Nana'* forms a very tight, neat mound shape. It is slow-growing enough for the base of a rockery where the soil does not dry out badly, or for a spot at the front of a border.

Above: Cryptomeria japonica *'Spiralis'* has spiralling locks of foliage that make young plants look rather like a wig. Do not allow it to dry out, or some stems will turn brown.

Cryptomeria japonica *'Lobbii'* has drooping tips to its stems. It was introduced by Thomas Lobb in the 1850s.

Above: Cryptomeria japonica *'Sekkan-Sugi'* has pale feathery foliage and eventually makes a dense medium to large, regular bushy shape; a good contrast for dark evergreens and red stems of dogwoods and heathers.

Cryptomeria japonica *'Sekkan-Sugi'* has sparse foliage that makes the stems look like soft whipcord.

Junipers for the rockery

Since junipers are relatively slow growing, it is quite feasible to grow them in pots for a few years before they need to be planted out into the garden. This means that a good collection of potted junipers - even those destined to grow big eventually - can be used temporarily to decorate a paved area or, by plunging pots to their rims, in raised beds or rockeries. (If used temporarily, leaving the plants in pots is essential, as junipers dislike being dug up and moved once they are permanently planted.) By using a good range of cultivars with distinctive shapes and colors, it is not difficult to create an interesting year-round display that can be augmented by seasonal additions, such as tubs of agapanthus, alpines, dwarf bulbs, grasses and other plants that associate well with them. However, for permanent planting in raised beds or rockeries where space is short, it is essential to choose cultivars that are very slow growing or remain naturally small and compact, since junipers

Above: Juniperus squamata *'Blue Star' certainly lives up to its name, with twinkling blue foliage borne on a small, star-shaped bush when young. With age, it spreads slowly to make a low, ground-hugging mat.*

Juniperus squamata *'Blue Star' makes a dense, rather prickly bush like a craggy dome with spiky steely blue foliage. It stays compact at about 18x18in (45x45cm) in 10 years.*

Growing bulbs with dwarf conifers

Avoid teaming dwarf conifers and rock plants with bulbs, since bulbs need a dry resting period while they are dormant, unlike conifers, which must be kept just moist all year round to avoid foliage browning. If you want to use bulbs in containers, use dwarf species to keep them in scale, grow them in a pot and sink this temporarily into a vacant spot in the container. It is then easy to lift the pot out when the flowers are over and replace it with something else.

cannot be kept small by pruning. *Juniperus communis* 'Compressa', *Juniperus squamata* 'Blue Star' and *J. s.* 'Meyeri' are amongst the best for this use. They provide good all-year-round backgrounds to a changing succession of rock plants throughout the season - dwarf spring bulbs, sedums, saxifrages and sempervivums, but avoid invasive plants, such as aubretia, that tend to swamp plants round them.

Junipers need to grow in full sun and soon deteriorate if smothered by creeping plants or weeds. Where more space is available, any of the medium-sized junipers can be used to maintain the contrast in shape and size between conifers and other inhabitants of the dry bed. And horizontal, ground-covering junipers could be used to cascade down over the edge of a raised bed or drop wall, or to soften the edge of steps.

Juniperus communis 'Compressa' is one of the most tolerant and popular rock garden conifers, rarely reaching 3ft(90cm) high, even when it is quite elderly. It forms a neat upright cone with very dense tidy foliage.

Junipers in tubs

Junipers make good year-round patio plants. For a tub, choose compact, slow-growing species, such as 'Blue Star' and 'Compressa'. Cover the drainage hole in the base with crocks and fill the tub with soil-based potting mix. Knock the junipers out of their pots and plant them with drought-tolerant rock plants to cover the soil surface and cascade over the sides of the pot.

Above: J. communis *'Compressa' is ideal for rockeries; it tolerates poor, hot dry soil, and grows slowly to make a perfect conical shape roughly 18in(45cm) high after ten years.*

Right: Juniperus squamata *'Meyeri' is another tough but attractive cultivar. It makes a small bushy shape of wiry steel-blue foliage and is perfect for rockeries, patios and gravel gardens.*

Ground cover junipers

Junipers are a large, attractive family of conifers, whose members include tall pencil shapes, compact flame shapes, low spreading and totally prostrate carpeters, in a range of foliage colors including shades of green, gold, gray and blue. Their ability to withstand poor dry soil without going brown makes them an asset in 'difficult' situations, such as poor stony soil, on rockeries, raised beds and banks, patios, in gaps between paving and in containers, where other conifers would soon suffer. The low spreading junipers are particularly useful for ground cover. Cultivars of *Juniperus* x *media* grow into fascinating abstract shapes that look good in small beds in a patio, set against paving slabs, or in a gravel bed with a similar 'hard' background. Grow them in beds, rising from a carpet of low heathers or glossy evergreen ground-covering plants such as *Gaultheria procumbens*, or team them with tall upright shapes, such as *Juniperus scopulorum* 'Skyrocket', birches or pines. Or create an interesting group using these with one of the ultra-flat *Juniperus horizontalis* cultivars. Although junipers do grow in poor conditions, they thrive in better soil. Low-growing and prostrate junipers make very effective ground cover, supplying foliage colors and textures that contrast well with adjacent groups of heathers and evergreens, and they show off more striking specimen conifers to perfection.

Above: Juniperus communis *'Effusa' is less common than the well-known conical species, but is most attractive. It is grown for its exceptionally neat and tidy, low spreading habit.*

Juniperus horizontalis *'Andorra Compacta'. Once they cover the ground, horizontal junipers create a dense layer that smothers out weeds. Fallen foliage under the plants contributes to the weed supressant effect, while automatically mulching the plants.*

The foliage of Juniperus communis *'Effusa' is silvery beneath.*

Above: *Junipers are famed for their ability to put up with inhospitable, hot dry conditions. This makes spreading kinds, such as this Juniperus horizontalis, ideal for edging a heather bed bordered by a gravel path.*

Juniperus davurica expansa 'Variegata', *a dwarf plant with thick horizontal branches, eventually makes a low, ground-hugging mound. After 10 years it is about 1ft(30cm) high and 3ft(90cm) across. The foliage is dappled with creamy-white variegations.*

Above: *Spreading junipers also make a good, low-maintenance ground cover 'link' between garden features, such as paths and a lawn. This is J. squamata 'Blue Carpet'; use it for any 'difficult' spot in dry sun.*

Juniperus horizontalis, *the popular creeping juniper, has a number of cultivars of various colors. All are good, tolerant plants that put up with extremes of heat, drought and cold without browning. The branches trail slightly, making the plant good for growing on a problem bank or over a low wall.*

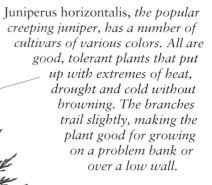

Medium-sized junipers

Junipers that reach 4-6ft(1.2-2m) tall in ten years are a bit too large for small rock gardens and raised beds, and can be expected to outgrow pots after a few years. However, they are very useful in the general garden, where a bigger plant is needed, but one that will not outgrow its welcome. Use medium-sized junipers on banks, rocky outcrops, gravel gardens or as the main conifer plantings in gardens on sandy or gravelly soils. Since junipers thrive in the better conditions favored by other choosier conifers, you can also grow them in evergreen gardens or those based on heathers and conifers. Some of the best varieties in this middle range group have interesting shapes and foliage textures. *Juniperus communis* 'Gold Cone', for example, makes a narrow, upright shape rather like a fastigiate golden yew, but smaller; the foliage is strikingly similar. *Juniperus communis* 'Golden Showers' has almost fluffy foliage and makes a flame shape. *Juniperus media* 'Plumosa Aurea' makes an informal, open, bushy shape, with feathery gold-green foliage. The best known narrow pencil-shaped juniper is *J. scopulorum* 'Skyrocket', whose foliage is steely blue-gray; *Juniperus communis* 'Hibernica' makes a similar shape, but with densely packed deep green foliage. Both are slow growers that reach 6-8ft (2-2.5m) in ten years. They continue to grow, but their narrow girth means that they do not take up any more room, and the contrast in shape makes them well worth including. But if you fall for a juniper that will ultimately grow bigger than the available space, simply keep it trimmed regularly and when it finally outgrows the spot, replace it rather than butcher it.

Above: Junipers come in an incredible range of shapes and colors; Juniperus chinensis 'Kuriwao Gold' makes an irregular bushy shape, boldly splashed with gold, that teams well with strong upright or low spreading shapes.

Juniperus chinensis 'Kuriwao Gold'

Juniperus x media 'Pfitzeriana Aurea'

Right: Juniperus scopulorum 'Skyrocket' heads for blast off. The striking shape makes most impact when these junipers are grouped in threes or fives in a large border. Where it is happy, it can reach a height of 12ft(3.7m) or more in ten years, although on poor dry soil it is slower growing.

Juniperus scopulorum 'Skyrocket'

Above: Low spreading junipers can be used in many unusual and artistic ways around the garden. Here, Juniperus x media *'Aurea' has been teamed with the foxy-foliage of* Spiraea bumalda *'Gold Flame' to create an unusually striking plant association.*

Juniperus x media 'Aurea'

Dwarf spruces

For situations where space is short, choose naturally small members of the spruce family, whose fascinating shapes and textures perfectly complement any small heather and conifer feature or rock garden. The small, neat, dense conical shapes of *Picea glauca albertiana* 'Conica' are so geometrically precise they look like topiary, but without the need for trimming. Though they can eventually reach 6ft(2m) high and perhaps 39in(1m) across, they are so slow-growing that it takes many years for them to reach even half this size. A feature of this cultivar is the fresh green spring growth set against the deeper mossy green background of old leaves; a second 'flush' of growth can occur in late summer given favorable weather. A new cultivar, 'Alberta Blue', is a sport from *P. g. albertiana* 'Conica', having a similar shape, growth rate and density but with good, blue spruce-colored foliage. Both this and 'Conica' make good plants for pots on the patio, and for temporary use indoors as reusable live Christmas trees. Look out for compact forms of *Picea pungens*, which includes many compact cultivars with blue or blue-gray foliage, as well as the bigger and better known blue spruces. *Picea pungens* 'Prostrata' is a good blue-leaved form, like a blue spruce but with branches arranged from a horizontal trunk instead of a vertical one; it makes a superb contrast with heathers, with the big bonus of casting very little shade, so you can use it near the front of a heather bed. Short, squat globular shapes, such as *Picea pungens* 'Globosa', a blue-gray form, add a colorful geometric note without taking up much room. Less easy to find is a striking dwarf spruce, *Picea mariana* 'Nana', a tightly packed blue-gray globular plant, blue-tinged in summer. It only reaches about 12in(30cm) high when fully grown, so team it with small alpine plants to ensure that it is not swamped.

Above: *A very neat, self-forming architectural shape is that of* Picea abies 'Nidiformis', *which looks like a bird's nest; the plant often grows with a depressed center that makes the name even more apt.*

Picea abies 'Nidiformis' *makes a wide, spreading, deep green plant that looks as if it has grown in layers. It grows to 1ft(30cm) high and 2ft(60cm) across in ten years.*

Left: Picea glauca albertiana 'Conica' has been a popular cultivar for many years. Although extremely slow-growing, old specimens at 6-8ft (2-2.5m) may begin to broaden out; young plants reach 3ft(90cm) high in ten years.

Right: The low spreading shape of Picea mariana 'Nana' makes a good contrast in texture and color amongst a carpet of heathers, and helps to brighten the bed even when the surrounding plants are not in flower.

Picea glauca albertiana 'Conica' grows into a neat, densely packed pyramid with bright green new growth in spring.

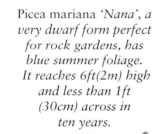

Picea mariana 'Nana', a very dwarf form perfect for rock gardens, has blue summer foliage. It reaches 6ft(2m) high and less than 1ft (30cm) across in ten years.

Picea glauca albertiana 'Alberta Globe' is a rounded form with bright green spring foliage. It reaches 2ft(60cm) high in 10 years.

Above: Prune out upright-growing shoots that appear in prostrate forms of blue spruce, such as this Picea pungens 'Glauca Prostrata', or the plant may revert to an upright habit.

Blue spruces

Spruces are a large group of conifers that include many beautiful kinds suitable for smaller gardens. The blue spruces (*Picea pungens* cultivars, such as 'Hoto', 'Koster' and 'Hoopsii') are particularly spectacular, with rich coloring that lasts all year round. Some even have a silver-frosted effect that makes them look as if the foliage has been sprinkled with snow. Blue spruces are slow growing but in time become rather bigger than many of the conifers recommended for small gardens, so take care when siting them. They make imposing specimen trees for the middle of a lawn or as a centerpiece to a conifer and heather bed. If they outgrow their space, the best solution is to fell them, remove the stumps and replant, rather than pruning to make them fit the space, as this ruins the shape. Blue spruces can also be grown in pots for quite a few years. Since they are slow growing and the effect of the container is to keep the root system restricted, a potted plant stays naturally smaller and more compact than the same plant would be when grown in the ground. Potgrown blue spruces make sensational living Christmas trees. You can bring such a potted tree indoors for two weeks without harm (a cool room is best), then gradually reacclimatize it to conditions outdoors or put it in an unheated greenhouse till spring, then stand it out in the garden for the summer. In this way, the same tree can be reused for several years until it grows too big to take indoors. After this, you can plant it outside in the garden and decorate it with outdoor lights for the festive season. Blue spruces grow well in most reasonable soil so long as they do not dry out badly in summer; avoid very exposed, windy sites to see the foliage at its best.

Right: Picea pungens 'Globosa' *makes a dense, squat, conical shape, with pale blue, 'hoar-frosted' foliage. It is one of the more slow growing and compact of the blue spruces and ideal for pots or in a small garden.*

Right: Picea pungens 'Hoopsii' *is the ultimate blue spruce, with a built-in silver-frosted effect on the foliage. Broader at the base than 'Koster', it not only makes the perfect 'designer' Christmas tree, but also a brilliant specimen tree for pride of place in the garden.*

Even as young plants in pots at the garden center, blue spruces exhibit their typical shape. 'Hoopsii' has wider-spaced branches than 'Globosa' and a more upright pyramidal shape.

Picea pungens 'Globosa' appears much squatter and denser than 'Hoopsii'.

Above: Picea pungens 'Koster' is symmetrical in shape and a good clear silvery-blue color that lasts well all year. Although tall eventually, it takes ten years to reach 6-9ft(2-2.8m)

Christmas trees

The traditional Christmas tree is Norway spruce (*Picea abies*), which tends to shed needles badly, even if you grow a live tree with roots in a pot instead of the usual cut specimen. Suppliers are increasingly getting round the problem by selling the costlier Noordman spruce *(Abies noordmanniana),* which looks similar but retains its needles better. However, plenty of prettier conifers make good 'alternative' Christmas trees. Those with pyramidal shapes and well-spaced branches that leave room for attaching pendant decorations are best, though some close-packed compact varieties are suitable, too; these are best decorated with strings of colored beads or simple ornaments laid on the outside. Blue spruces are firm favorites, since the foliage is a striking color and many varieties have a silvery sparkle that looks like frost. *Abies koreana*, the Korean fir, makes a loose pyramid that is easy to decorate but in any case produces violet cones, even on young trees. Conical piceas, such as *Picea glauca albertiana* 'Conica', make small, neat, compact, dense shapes suitable for small rooms. By leaving Christmas conifers in pots, you can reuse them each year until they grow too big to bring indoors. Even then, you can plant them out in the garden and decorate them with lights. The secret of keeping a live Christmas tree is to bring it indoors at the last moment, keep it in a cool room, and return it outdoors on Twelfth Night. By then it will have become acclimatized to indoor conditions, so keep it in a very sheltered place or, better still, a cold green-house to 'harden off' again gradually. In northern climes, if you put it straight out into the cold from a warm room, the shock could cause needle drop or severe browning. When the spring flush of growth starts, repot it into a pot one size larger, with fresh, soil-based potting mix. Keep it well watered and regularly fed, and plunge it to the rim in a sunny garden border or stand it on a patio as background foliage for your summer-flowering tubs.

Picea pungens 'Erich Frahm' is a popular blue spruce cultivar that makes a broadly conical shape reaching 7-8ft (2.1-2.5m) high and 3ft(90cm) across at the base in ten years. It needs reasonable soil, sun and shelter.

The neat, perfectly pyramidal habit of Picea glauca albertiana 'Conica' makes it ideal as an unusual Christmas tree. Grows to 3ft(90cm) high and 1ft(30cm) wide at the base in ten years.

Being a live plant growing with all its roots, Picea orientalis 'Gracilis' is unlikely to shed its needles unless it dries out badly. It is slow growing, but eventually makes quite a big tree, 16-20ft(5-6m) high. Growing it in a pot will keep it compact.

Above: *The traditional Christmas tree, Norway spruce, is sold with cut roots. You can reduce its natural tendency to shed needles by spraying it with an anti-transpirant spray (sold as Christmas tree spray at the start of the festive season) before bringing the tree indoors. Water trees regularly to reduce needle drop, but always unplug the lights first and avoid getting water on electrical fittings.*

Right: *A live Christmas tree (Picea abies), complete with roots, can be kept growing from one year to the next simply by planting it out into the garden after Twelfth Night. Alternatively, plunge the pot to the rim in a border.*

Miniature pines

Of all the various conifers, miniature pines must be the most choice. Their dramatic craggy shapes (which become more distinctive with age) and often long, elegant needles give them great character. They are often in short supply and many varieties will always be rare, as they are slow and difficult to propagate - mostly by grafting - so they are normally cost a bit more than many conifers. Look out for them in the catalogs of mail-order nurseries that specialize in conifers or when visiting a conifer specialist, as most garden centers only stock a fairly limited selection. Dwarf pines are mostly very slow-growing and remain compact for many years. They are good candidates for growing in favored situations in pots on patios, raised beds and rock gardens, but are happy in a border as long as they are not smothered by surrounding plants - pines need plenty of sun and fresh air. Although they are relatively robust, it makes sense to give them a bit more care, so make sure they have well-drained soil that does not dry out too severely and some organic matter. As dwarf pines are so slow-growing, and it will take a long time to remedy any shape defects, it pays to pick healthy, well-shaped specimens in the first place. Look for good, clear foliage without any brown needles or bald patches, and a good shape; this need not be regular, as some varieties are naturally craggy from a young age, but choose an attractive specimen, as the basic shape will not change much as the plant gets older.

Pinus sylvestris 'Watereri' is a conical bush with upturning branches and bluish foliage that grows to 4ft(1.2m) in 10 years.

Pinus mugo 'Winter Gold' grows about 3ft(90cm) high and wide in ten years.

Pinus nigra 'Nana' has dark green foliage and a compact, rounded shape. It reaches 30in(75cm) in ten years.

Left: *Pinus mugo 'Winter Gold' grows slowly to make a dense bushy plant. Its bright gold-tipped shoots show up particularly well in winter.*

Right: *From l to r: Pinus leucodermis 'Satellit' is upright in shape and grows to 5ft(1.5m) in ten years. Pinus parviflora 'Negishi' dark green, roughly pyramidal and reaches 5ft (1.5m) in ten years. Pinus pumila 'Globe', a dwarf bushy plant for rock gardens, has blue-gray needles and cones from an early age. It grows just 2ft(60cm) in ten years.*

Pinus leucodermis 'Compact Gem' is pyramidal in shape and grows 3ft (90cm) high and wide in ten years.

Pinus parviflora 'Negishi'

Pinus leucodermis 'Satellit'

Pinus pumila 'Globe'

Pinus mugo 'Gnom', a compact dome-shaped pine, grows 2ft(60cm) across in 10 years and produces cones from an early age. Good for rock gardens.

Pinus mugo 'Humpy' is another very dwarf form suitable for rock gardens. It grows to 30in(75cm) in ten years.

Specimen pines

The pine family is a large one that includes some fascinating, highly architectural and garden-worthy trees of various sizes. Among the larger kinds are several that make superb specimen plants, perfect to add height to a heather and conifer bed or to grow in a lawn or Mediterranean-style garden. For modest-sized gardens, choose very slow-growing kinds, such as the extremely long-lived Bristlecone pines (*Pinus aristata*), and *Pinus coulteri,* which has the largest cones of any conifer (each weighing several pounds). Both can be accommodated in normal gardens for very many years before they outgrow their space. Use pots to restrict the growth rate and size of dramatic but slightly tender exotic pines, such as *Pinus patula* and *Pinus montezumae,* whose most striking characteristic is their very long needles. Both originate from the Mexico area so are not hardy in any but the mildest regions, although they make very good pot specimens for the patio in summer and conservatory in winter. In very exposed or coastal gardens, a combination of rocky or sandy soil and strong winds will help to restrict the growth of the shapely but rugged *Pinus radiata,* (the Monterey pine), *Pinus thunbergii* and *Pinus nigra* 'Maritima'. These can either be grown as single specimens or planted in rows as a windbreak. Another pine that tolerates hotter summers and poorer, dryer soil conditions is *Pinus pinea*. Where the shape of a specimen pine is needed but size must be carefully controlled, you can regulate even the very hardy kinds by growing them in pots and carrying out annual root pruning. Be sure to water them regularly in summer to prevent drying out. They are one of the most popular bonsai subjects.

Below: Pinus pinea *makes a regular umbrella shape. It is good for warm, dry, sandy regions, but despite its warm origins, it is hardy enough to grow in cooler climates, too.*

Above: A row of Pinus radiata *planted as a windbreak acts as a first line of defense against strong salt-laden winds in coastal areas.*

Pine nuts

Pine nuts are the seeds from the ripe cones of several species of pine from warm climates. They have a soft waxy texture and mild nutty taste and are widely used in Mediterranean cookery.

There are many named cultivars of the Austrian pine, one of the most rugged species suitable for windy coastal situations and limy soils. This one is Pinus nigra 'Bright Eyes'.

Left: Pinus sylvestris 'Moseri' is one of the compact forms of Scots pine. It makes a dense, compact, regular shape that will not outgrow the average garden. Unlike the much bigger Scots pine, this one keeps its trunk covered.

Pinus sylvestris 'Moseri'. There are several cultivars of Scots pine, which mainly arose from witches brooms, but are considerably more compact than the type.

Below: Pinus aristata, the bristlecone pine, represents good value for money - it is one of the longest lived trees on earth! Specimens over 2,000 years old survive in the southern states of the USA.

Yews for hedging

English yew *(Taxus baccata)* is the traditional tree of churchyards, and supplied the flexible timber used to make longbows. For many centuries, it was widely used for long-lived hedging and elaborate topiary shapes. (The oldest living yew tree is believed to be four thousand years old.) Yew hedging is the traditional favorite for backing herbaceous borders at stately homes, and is also trained to make arbors. Overgrown or neglected yew hedges can be cut back far closer than most plants would tolerate; an old hedge can be rejuvenated by cutting it back virtually to the trunks in early summer. (It is a good idea to tackle only one side of the hedge at a time. Treat the other side a couple of years later, when the original area has made a covering of new growth.) Yew is also the plant used for large topiary specimens that need internal support; heavy iron frames were traditionally used. However, small topiary can be left self-supporting or given a light framework of wire netting. Unlike most conifers, yew roots quite easily from cuttings, making it feasible to grow your own hedge very cheaply. Rooted cuttings need 'stopping' frequently to encourage them to develop the dense branching structure essential for a hedge that is solid right to the base, with no bases of trunks showing. Yew hedges are traditionally 'bantered' - clipped so that the top slopes in slightly. This allows rainwater to reach the roots of the hedge better, as there is no overhang to deflect it away. Sloping sides also encourage snow to slide off in winter, instead of building up until the weight makes the plants splay open, spoiling the shape of the hedge. Despite being slow growing, yew does not take as long as you would think to become established as a hedge. Young plants are much faster growing than old ones; it is the established hedge that grows slowly. Clip it twice a year in early and late summer for a good-looking but low-maintenance barrier that is a real investment in the garden.

Poisonous berries

The leaves and seeds of yew are both poisonous, although the flesh of the berry is not. This explains why birds are able to eat them safely, since they only digest the flesh - the seeds pass straight through them. Livestock and humans can, however, easily be poisoned, which is why, despite its toughness, yew is not used as a countryside hedge, only around gardens.

Right: Yew makes a very versatile hedge. It does not have to be grown in the traditional formal straight line bordering a garden. It can also be used, as here, to create a gently curving edge to a large border.

Yew cuttings

Prepare yew cuttings in early fall and keep them in a cold frame or unheated greenhouse for the winter, watering lightly. Stand them outside in a cool shady spot in late spring and summer.

3 In mid- to late summer, cut back all shoots to 1-2in(2.5-5cm) from the main stem to encourage side shoots from the base of the trunk.

4 Two years from taking the cutting, you have a dense, bushy plant ready for planting for hedging or to train into topiary shapes.

1 Take 6-8in(15-20cm) cuttings from shoot tips. Nip out growing points. Root them into 3.5in(9cm) pots of seed mixture with 25% grit.

2 Start liquid feeding in midsummer, when plenty of new roots should be present and new growth is appearing.

Above: *Yew topiary creates a fun-but-formal look without a lot of work. Once the basic shape is formed, the finished result only needs trimming twice a year.*

Left: *A traditional country garden with herbaceous borders backed by yew hedges. It is a good idea to leave a bare strip of ground between the back of the border and the hedge for easy access when clipping.*

Specimen yews

Although yews are normally thought of as plants for hedging or topiary, there are several more unusual striking 'architectural' kinds that make wonderful slow-growing specimen plants. Give them pride of place in a garden or perhaps use them to accentuate a feature such as an entrance, arch or doorway. Unlike many conifers, yews are quite tolerant of poor chalky soils (a talent they share with junipers), and will even put up with some shade, although this is not advisable for gold or variegated cultivars. They do need well-drained conditions to thrive, however. Upright-growing, spire-shaped varieties, described as 'fastigiate', are the best known of the 'specimen' yews. These include the Irish Yew *(Taxus baccata)*, which naturally makes a tall lean column of deep green, and its more spectacular gold forms, popularly known as golden Irish yews. These make dense golden columns with deeper green highlights created by slight variations in color between young and old foliage. Upright yews can be used wherever a strong upright shape is need, and look specially stunning planted in a double row as a yew 'avenue' leading up to a formal garden.

Forms of *Taxus baccata* 'Dovastoniana' are not so well known and create totally different shapes - while young, these yews are upright bushy plants with branches in tiers with weeping tips. With age, they form more relaxed wide-spreading bushy plants. Again, they make very striking shapes for a focal point in the garden, and both green and gold forms are available. Like all yews, those mentioned here take very kindly to trimming, so there is no excuse for plants to grow out of shape. But they are too expensive to use as topiary, especially when normal yew does so well.

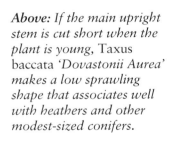

Above: If the main upright stem is cut short when the plant is young, Taxus baccata 'Dovastonii Aurea' makes a low sprawling shape that associates well with heathers and other modest-sized conifers.

Taxus baccata 'Dovastonii Aurea'. Remove any upright stems to maintain a low shape.

Taxus baccata 'Dovastoniana' makes a low spreading tree, with elegant drooping branches growing in tiers, unless it loses its central leader, when it tends to become urn-shaped.

Like 'Aureomarginata', Taxus baccata 'Fastigiata Robusta' reaches about 6ft(2m) in ten years and makes a good specimen for the garden. In common with hedging yews, this cultivar tolerates some shade.

Trim and shape

All yews take kindly to clipping and shaping; the types shown here naturally grow into striking shapes that make them suitable for use as specimen plants, but judicious tying in and clipping help to accentuate the shapes.

1 *Create a more pronounced pillar shape by spiralling green plastic-coated flexible wire loosely around the main branches.*

2 *Maintain a clean outline by clipping. This encourages side shoots, which will thicken up the plant and produce upright stems.*

Taxus baccata 'Fastigiata Aureomarginata'. Here, the dark green leaves are edged with yellow, giving a golden glow when seen from a distance. Yew berries are poisonous, but 'Aureomarginata' is a male form that does not produce any, so it is perhaps the best choice if children and pets have access to the garden.

Taxus baccata 'Standishii' is slow growing and ideal for containers or small gardens. The two golden yews need plenty of sun to develop their full color.

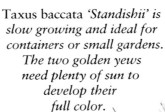

Below: *Taxus baccata 'Standishii' makes an architectural pillar shape that looks at home parallel to a doorway or, as here, a window.*

Thujas for hedging

Thujas (whose common name is arbor-vitae, the romantic sounding 'tree of life') include two species commonly used for hedging - *Thuja occidentalis* and *Thuja plicata*. Both make far more suitable hedges for small gardens than fast-growing conifers, such as Leyland's cypress *(Cupressocyparis leylandii)*. They do not grow as tall (although when allowed to develop naturally they still make fair-sized trees), so when grown as a hedge, they need less work to keep them at a suitable size - even though they take longer to get up to the required height in the first place. *Thuja plicata* and *occidentalis* are plain green conifers that are propagated in bulk for hedging and sold cheaply. Choose *plicata* if you want a tall hedge and *occidentalis* for one under 6ft(2m). However, if you only require a small amount of hedging and want to achieve a 'special' result, use one of the many named cultivars instead. These will be more expensive than hedging kinds. For example, colored compact varieties, such as 'Rheingold', when planted in a row and left unclipped make a nice natural undulating hedge that suggests it has been formed naturally by wind-pruning, as you sometimes see in the countryside. Compact, named varieties are those to go for if you want a low, easy-care hedge - *Thuja plicata* 'Rogersii', for example, reaches 10ft(3m) in 10 years. Before planting a hedge, it is always worth improving the soil, as it is the only chance you will have. Excavate a deep trench and mix plenty of well-rotted organic matter plus general fertilizer into the soil used to backfill around the roots. Put in the plants about 2ft(60cm) apart, and water in well. Do not neglect hedges after planting; they benefit from routine care in the same way as conifers in a border. Feed them each spring with a general fertilizer and mulch with a 1in(2.5cm) layer of well-rotted organic matter while the soil is moist. Clip conifer hedges, even young ones, as this stimulates branching growth that thickens them up. Do this twice a year, in early and late summer, to keep them neat with minimal effort.

Conifers for hedging

Select specimens as similar as possible. Avoid any that are misshapen or with brown patches; poor specimens never grow strongly and any that die will leave gaps in the hedge that new plants will take time to fill.

The top of this Thuja plicata 'Rogersii' *has died and spoilt the shape.*

A well-shaped specimen with fresh, healthy foliage.

Left: The 'turrets' cut into this thuja hedge provide interesting detail and turn what could easily be a purely functional screen (perhaps hiding an unsightly oil tank) into a decorative architectural feature.

Right: Thuja plicata *makes a good hedge that keeps its color during winter and responds well to training. The dramatic shape - added to give detail to the small front garden - is emphasized here by the fall of snow.*

The 'windows' in this thuja hedge leave a reasonable amount of privacy, but allow more light to reach the garden and also prevent the hedge acting as cover for vandals or intruders

Thuja occidentalis 'Smaragd'

Thuja plicata 'Zebrina'

Left: *Although more expensive than plain thuja hedging, named varieties will give a hedge with more interesting foliage. By choosing relatively small varieties, you can control the ultimate size of the hedge, making it less work to look after.*

Thuja occidentalis 'Holmstrupii'

Thujas for the rockery

At first glance, thujas can easily be mistaken for chamaecyparis. The plants make similar shapes and both have flattened sprays of foliage made up of wiry stems clad in tiny, pointed, scalelike leaves. But you can tell them apart in an instant, as thujas have aromatic foliage that is noticeable when you squeeze a handful of leaves. Thujas are a much smaller 'family' of conifers than chamaecyparis, but there are no really tiny cultivars. Nevertheless, they contain many attractive and useful small- to medium-sized cultivars, any of which are suitable for large rock gardens or well-drained borders with other plants. The smallest thujas reach 2 or 3ft (60 or 90cm) after ten years, and these compact cultivars combine interesting shapes, colors and foliage textures with sufficiently strong growth to allow you to plant them safely in a carpet of heathers or ground cover plants without fear of them being swamped. Compact thujas also have the great advantage of being popular and readily available everywhere. Various named cultivars are available in a good range of shapes except narrow, upright pillars. There are cultivars with flattened sprays of fanlike foliage and a neat domed shape, such as *T. orientalis* 'Aurea Nana', and those with looser pyramidal shapes and feathery foliage, such as *T. occidentalis* 'Rheingold'. Thujas are easy to grow and thrive in most reasonable soils, as long as they are well drained; they cannot tolerate waterlogging. They will also take a little light shade, which few conifers are happy to grow in, but do not attempt to grow any of the colored leaf kinds in anything but full sun or their color fades to a very unhealthy looking, washed-out pallor and they will not grow well.

Thuja occidentalis *'Danica'* grows into a dense globular shape, with foliage in flattened upright sprays.

Thuja occidentalis *'Sunkist'* is a newer variety with gold-touched ends to the green foliage.

Left: *When grown in an open, sunny situation, the color of the slow-growing* Thuja occidentalis *'Rheingold' develops fully to the foxy auburn shade that makes the plant so popular. This plant is virtually full-sized.*

Thuja occidentalis 'Rheingold' is a broad bushy conical plant, with a loose feathery habit. The reddish-tinged gold foliage gives the overall impression of amber.

Thuja orientalis 'Aurea Nana' is a compact, dense, bushy plant, roughly globular, with upright fans of gold foliage.

Right: Thuja orientalis 'Aurea Nana' is probably one of the most distinctive small conifers. In texture it consists of rows of overlapping 'fans' of foliage and makes a neat, dumpy bush. Good drainage is essential for success.

Index to Plants

Page numbers in **bold** indicate major text references. Page numbers in *italics* indicate captions and annotations to photographs. Other text entries are shown in normal type.

Credits

The majority of the photographs featured in this book have been taken by Neil Sutherland and are © Colour Library Books. The publishers wish to thank the following photographers for providing additional photographs, credited here by page number and position on the page, i.e. (B)Bottom, (T)Top, (C)Center, (BL)Bottom left, etc.

Bruce Coleman: 82(BC, Jeremy Grayson)
Eric Crichton: Half-title, 13(R), 46(TR), 52(T), 53(R), 54(BL), 57(C,BR), 63(BL), 64(TR), 65(TC), 67(C, BR), 68(TR), 69(TL,TR), 70(TR), 71(TC,TR), 73(TL,BR), 75(T), 77(BR), 78(TR), 81(TC,BC), 82-3(TC), 83(BL), 84(TR), 85(BR), 89(R)
John Feltwell, Garden Matters: 80(BC)
Garden Picture Library: 10(Brigitte Thomas), 62(TR, Neil Holmes), 63(R, Brian Carter), 72(TR, Jerry Pavia), 74(J.S. Sira), 82(BR, Marijke Heuff, photographer, Mrs M. van Bennekorn, designer), 86(B, Guy Bouchet), 99(TR, Howard Rice)
John Glover: Copyright page, 25(BR), 26(T), 27(TC), 45(TC), 46(TL), 47(T), 56(TR), 58(TR), 62(BR), 65(TR)
Holt Studios/Nigel Cattlin, 20(BR), 21(BC)
S & O Mathews: 44(TL,TR), 55(L,TR), 62(BL), 73(TR)
Clive Nichols: 23(R, Chiffchaffs, Dorset), 24(T, Graham Strong), 43(TL, Yew Tree Cottage, Sussex), 75(BL, Greenhurst Garden, Sussex)
Photos Horticultural: 45(BL), 53(TL), 57(TR), 59(TC,TR), 66(TR), 80(TR), 87(T)

Acknowledgments

The publishers would like to thank the following people and organizations for providing plants and/or photographic facilities during the production of this book: Bridgemere Garden World, Nantwich, Cheshire; Court Lane Nursery, Hadlow College, Kent; Hillier Nurseries (Winchester) Ltd., Romsey, Hampshire; Murrells Nursery, Pulborough, West Sussex.